THE INCREDIBLE LITTLE BOOK OF

10,001

NAMES FOR HORSES

BY BARBARA MANNIS & CATHERINE LEWIS

PUBLISHED BY HORSE HOLLOW PRESS, INC.

Many thanks to my husband, Fred, who patiently
allowed me to awaken him countless times a night as
I thought of names that I knew I'd forget by morning. I'd turn
on the light, reach for a pen and paper, write down the names,
turn off the light, and repeat this process again and again,
knowing from experience that if you write in the dark, you
can't read a word in the daylight. (Fred also contributed the
following horse names — "A Million Laughs", "Replaceable You",
"Go to Sleep!" and "The Widower" — Does that explain
what was going on in his mind?) Also, special thanks to
my horse friends and other world friends, especially Donna
and Lauren, who listened, contributed, and encouraged.
—*Barbara Mannis*

I want to thank my three daughters for assisting me
with this project: Nicole Meehan (my oldest daughter)
for her help and guidance. Kristin and Morgan Lewis
(my youngest daughter) for their moral support. Thank you
Tom, my husband, for allowing me the space and free time
to finish this project. And, thank you Lisa Dobson, the
District Commisioner of the Redwoods Pony Club, for her
continued support and encouragement. And, last but not
least, thank you to my twin sister, Christie Bittner,
for all her added creativity.
—*Catherine Lewis*

TABLE OF CONTENTS

Barbara Mannis, of Malvern, Pennsylvania, rides her horse, Sky's The Limit (Skylar) in the Adult Amateur Divisions when she is not developing computer systems as a computer consultant in the finance and insurance industries.

Photo by Alix Coleman.

I am probably the least creative person you will ever meet. My drawings are all stick figures and the only "cooking" I do is in the microwave, but I have always enjoyed words and phrases and no pun was ever wasted on me.

My friends have always asked me to help name their horses. It started with one friend whose new horse arrived with the name Bo Winkle. She wanted to call him Bo, but preferred a more sophisticated name for the Adult Amateur show ring. After a few suggestions from me, she settled on Beau Geste, a very appropriate name for this debonair gentleman. My favorite is probably for my friend who purchased an Appendix Quarter Horse. He has a very large number 2 tatttoed on his side and is obviously callled "Two-ee" around the barn. She asked for ideas and I said I'd think about it and get back to her. My mind was spinning with possibilities and finally I had the perfect name. Appropriately, I called

her at two a.m. to suggest "Two-riffic". She loved the name and he has lived up to it two hundred fold over the past years.

I once read an article that said the happiest people are those who earn their living working with something they love. I love horses but no one will ever pay me to train them or their horse, and my barn management skills leave something to be desired. The next best thing seemed to be to write down the names as I thought of them and share them with others in "book form".

There are no guarantees that the names on these pages do not already belong to a horse you own or know. Actually if your horse's name is in here, it only proves that we agree it is a great name. And if you need a name, I hope you find one in here that is a perfect fit. Hmmmmmh "Perfect Fit" — what a great name for a horse. Maybe I will start thinking about Volume II.

—Barbara Mannis

A LITTLE NOTE FROM THE AUTHORS

I have always wanted to put down on paper all those clever horse names that I had been accumulating in my brain for years. Everytime I got an idea, I would say to my kids, "Wouldn't that make a great name for a horse?" They would reply, "Mom, is that all you think about?" I denied it for years, but have come to grips with the fact that I am obsessed with naming horses and ponies.

When my oldest daughter announced that she was expecting our first grandchild. My first response was, "What will the name be?" I immediately bought her a baby name book. There were hundreds of books devoted to baby names. Then, I thought to myself, "There is no such thing as a name book for horses?" Bingo, the light went on in my head and I went into high gear.

The first day I scribbled down 400 names on little pieces of paper that I had scattered all around the house. Everyday, I added hundreds more names. New horse names appeared to me in signs, billboards, advertisements, my kids, etc. I connected names together to form more names. I lit my computer on fire going through the names, changing them, adding to them. Names for colors, literary names, movies—just about everything can be made into a terrific horse name.

I came up with 5,000 names for horses and have another 5,000 in my head. It was great fun putting this book together and I hope you will have as much fun reading it.
—Catherine Lewis

Catherine Lewis of Petaluma, California, enjoys trail riding her appendix-bred Quarter Horse, Captain Marvel (Buddy). She is actively involved in her daughter's showing, lessons and Pony Club. She graduated from Nursing School in Cumberland, Maryland and, for the past 20 years, has been a Family Nurse Practitioner.

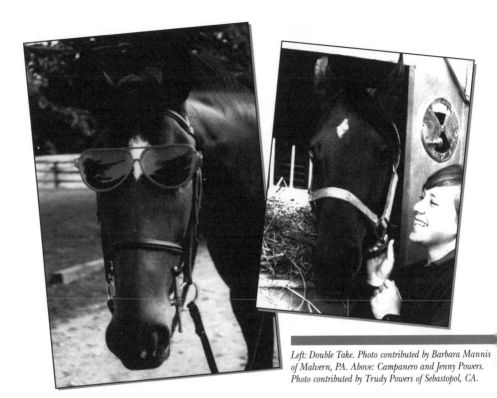

Left: Double Take. Photo contributed by Barbara Mannis of Malvern, PA. Above: Campanero and Jenny Powers. Photo contributed by Trudy Powers of Sebastopol, CA.

TIPS FOR NAME SELECTION

1. Use the specialized categories in this book as a guide, but feel free to choose any name (from any section) for your horse. Remember, if the name fits ...

2. You can add or subtract a word to a selected name in this book, or combine names, to invent your own.

3. You can also respell the chosen name the way it sounds; or capitalize a letter at the second syllable to accentuate it, such as GaZelle or JetSetter.

4. Consider names based on your horse's personality, appearance or athletic ability, conformation perfections or flaws (affectionately, of course!), coat colors, gender, sire & dam names, tradition or breed origins.

5. Tie in something that took place at foaling, such as a thunderstorm or snowfall, brilliant sunrise or sunset, an astrological or stellar event, even political or noteworthy incidents.

6. Name your horse after a famous actor, author, fictional character, or historical figure. The list here is endless.

7. Really stumped for a name? Try *The New Horse Name Game**. Write down various names, parts of names, and favorite words on separate slips of paper, and shuffle them in a bowl. Then pick out two or three slips at a time. Mix and match to create the best name.

The New Horse Name Game excerpted from *The Ultimate Guide to Pampering Your Horse*, published by Horse Hollow Press, Inc.

Yet-to-be named Standardbred yearling fillies.
Photo contributed by Dawn Lyons of
Montgomery, NY.

A

Abacus
Aberdeen
About Time
Abracadabra
Absatively Posalutely
Absent-Minded
Absent-Minded
    Professor
Absolute
Absolutely Positive
Abysmal
Abyss
Academia
Academy Award
A Calculated Move
Acceptable Risk
Acclamation
Accolade
Accounts Payable
Accounts Receivable

According To Hoyle
According To Protocol
Accrued Interest
Ace In The Hole
Ace Of Aces
A Certain Charm
Ace's High
Ace Up My Sleeve
Acey Ducey
Achilles
Ackerman
A Closer Look
Acoustic Blue
Acoustic Junction
Acrobat
Acrobatic Feat
Acrophobic
Acronym
Across The Board
Act Accordingly
Action Packed
Actions Speak Louder
    Than Words

Act Knowingly
Act Of Congress
Act Of Kindness
Acquaintance
Actor's Guild
Acute Angle
Added Comfort
Addendum
Addicted
Adequate Remedy
Adieu
A Different Approach
Ad Infinitum
Adirondack
Adler
Admissible Evidence
A Dream Come True
Adriatic Sea
Adroit
Adulation
Advanced Degree
Advance Ticket
Advance Warning

Advantage
Advantix
Adventurous
Advocator
Aerialist
Aerial Stunts
Aromatic
Aesop's Fable
Aesthetic Approach
Affair To Remember
Affidavit
Affinity
Affirmative Action
After All
After Dark
After Effects
After Eight
After Five
After Hours
Aftermath
Afternoon Delight
Aftershock
After The Fact

Afterthoughts
Against All Odds
Against The Law
Against The Tide
Against The Wall
Agenda Item
Ageless
Age Of Aquarius
Age Of Consent
Age Of Reason
A Good Example
A Good Thing
A Good Word
A Great Idea
Agreeable
Ahead Of Its Time
Ahead Of My Time
Ahead Of The Game
Ahead Of Time
Aide-De-Camp
Aim To Please
Ain't Misbehavin'
Ain't Nobody's Fool
Ain't No Heathen
Airborne

Airborne Express
Air Force One
Airforce Recruit
Airmail
Air Raid
Airship
Air Tight
Airtight Alibi
Air Transporter
Air Waves
Airway
A.K.A.
Akimbo
A Known Fact
Akron
Alabama Slammer
À La Carte
Aladdin's Lamp
À La Mode
Album Of The Year
Albuquerque
Al Capone
Alchemist
A Learning
    Experience

Alexander The Great
Algebra II
Alfalfa
Alfa Romeo
Algorithms
Alhambra
Alias
Alibi
A Likely Candidate
A Likely Story
A-List
A Living Doll
All American
All At Once
All Business
All Decked Out
Allegiance
Allegory
All Eyes On Me
All For One
All Inclusive
All In Due Time
All In Fun
All In Good Time
All In Stride

All In Time
All Is Fair
All Is Well
All Jazzed Up
All Mine
All My Pride
All Occasion
All Of The Above
All Or Nothing
All Politics
All Purpose
All Rules Applied
All Sales Final
All's Clear
All's Fair
All Spice
All Spiffed Up
All Systems Go
All Talk
All That Glitters
All That Jazz
All The Facts
All The Luck
All The Rage
All The Right Moves

All The Trimmings
All Time High
Alliance
Allure
Alluring
Allusive Butterfly
Alma Mater
Almay
Almighty Dollar
Almost For Sure
Almost Magic
Almost Mine
Almost Perfect
Along For The Ride
Alphabetical Order
Alphabet Soup
Alpha Romeo
Alrighty Then
Also Ran
Altered Aspirations
Alter Ego
Alternative Ways
A Lucky Thought
Always Thinking
Amaretto

Amateur Writer
A Matter Of Fact
Amazing Grace
Ambiance
Ambidextrous
Ambiguous
Ambitious
Ambrosia
A Media Event
Amendment
American Appeal
American Bandstand
American Crafted
American Express
American Graffiti
American Pie
American Tradition
Amethyst
Amethyst Sky
Amiable
Amicable
Amigo
A Million Laughs
Amnesia Victim
Amnesty

Among The Elite
Amoré
Ampersand
Amtrak
Anachronism
Anagram
Analogy
An American Hero
Anchor's Aweigh
Ancient Line
Andalusia
Andretti
And Then Some
An Educated Guess
Angelic
Angel's Image
An Honorable Choice
Animated Character
Annual Bonus
Annuity
Anonym
Anonymous
An Ordinary Day
Another Affair
Another Chance

Another Choice
Another Dimension
Another Dream
Another Glance
Another Image
Another Level
Another Mess
Another Perspective
Another Rainbow
Another Round
Another Story
Another Touch
Another World
Another Yankee
A Novel Idea
Ansel Adams
Answered Prayers
Answering Machine
Answerman
Answer The Call
Ante Up
Anticipation
Antigua
Antique Lace
Antiquity

11

Antonym
Any Day Now
Any Eventuality
Anything Can Happen
Anything Goes
A Passing Fancy
Aperitif
Aplomb
Apollo 11
Apparition
Appealing Ways
Appearance Counts
Appearing Nightly
Applause
Applause Please
Apple Cider
Apple Crisp
Apple Dumpling
Apple Sauce
Applied Art
Appropriately
    Dressed
April Flowers
April Fool
April In Paris

April Love
April Morning
April's Fool
April Shower
April Snow
Apropos
Aquamarine
Arabesque
Arch Rival
Arc One
Arctic Fury
Argonaut
Aria
Aristocrat
Aristotle
Arlington
Armani
Armed And
    Dangerous
Armstrong
Around The Bend
Around The World
Arrivaderci
Arrive In Style
Arrowroot

A Run For The Money
Art History
Art T. Fact
Art With A Heart
A.S.A.P.
Ascension
A Separate Peace
As I Am
As Is
Ask for Details
As Luck Has It
Aspen
Aspirations
Aspiring Artist
Assertive
Assertive Style
Assumed Name
Assumption
Assured
As Time Goes By
Asti Spumanti
Astonishing
Astonishing Fact
Astonishing Talent
Astounding Results

Astral Traveler
Astronaut
A-Student
As We Speak
As You Imagined
As You Like It
At A Glance
At Any Cost
At Arms Length
At Close Range
At Ease
Atlantis
Atlas
At Last
At Liberty
At Long Last
Atomic Rocket
At Random
A Treasure Trove
Attaboy
Attaché
Attainable
Attention Getter
Attention Please
Attention Seeker

Attention To Detail
At The Mall
Attila
Attitude Adjustment
Attorney General
At Wit's End
At Your Convenience
At Your Service
Audacious
Audubon
August Moon
Au Natural
Auspicious
Auspicious Beginning
Auspicious Occasion
Authentic
Authority Figure
Auto Focus
Autograph Hound
Autograph Seeker
Automation
Autumn Applause
Available
Avalon
A Vanishing Breed

Avant Guard
Avanti
Avenger
Aversion
Aversion To Details
Avignon
Avis
Avon Calling
Awakening
Award
Award Winner
A Way Out
A Way With Words
Awesome
A.W.O.L.
A Word To The Wise
A World Apart
A World Of Difference
A World Of Good

Babe
Baby Blues
Baby Boomer
Baby Grand
Babylon
Baby's Breath
Bacardi
Baccarat
Bachelor Buttons
Bachelor Pad
Back Court
Backgammon
Background Check
Back In Time
Backlog
Back Stage
Back Street
Back To Basics
Back To Earth
Backwoodsman
Badge Of Courage

Bag Of Tricks
Bahama Mama
Bail Bondsman
Bailey's Irish Cream
Bailiwick
Balanced Books
Balanced Budget
Balance Of Power
Balancing Act
Baldwin
Ballad
Ballistic
Ballyhoo
Bancroft
Bandanna
Bandit
Bandito
Bandwagon
Bank Account
Banker's Trust
Banking On You
Banknote
Bank On It
Bank On Me
Bankrupt

13

Banned In Boston
Banter
Barclay
Bar Code
Barfly
Bar Harbor
Bar None
Bare Essentials
Bare Necessity
Bargaining Chip
Bargaining Power
Barometer Rising
Barreling Down
Barrington
Barrister
Barrymore
Barstow
Bartender
Bartholomew
Barton
Bases Loaded
Basic Ingredients
Batman
Baton Rouge

Batteries Not
   Included
Battle Cry
Bayard
Beach Ball
Beach Boy
Beach Bum
Beach Music
Beacon Hill
Bean Counter
Beansprout
Bean Town
Bear Hug
Bear With Me
Beatnik
Beat Of The Drum
Beat The Clock
Beat The Odds
Beat The System
Be A Trooper
Beau Monde
Beaumont
Beaujolais
Beauregard
Beautiful Dreamer

Beauty Mark
Be Bopper
Because Why
Bechtel
Beckett
Becoming Airborne
Bedazzle
Bedford
Bed Of Roses
Bedtime Story
Beefcake
Bee Line
Been Around
Been There,
   Done That
Beeper
Beethoven
Before Taxes
Befuddled
Beggar
Beginner's Luck
Begonia
Beg Your Pardon
Behind The
   Eight Ball

Behind The Scenes
Bel Air
Belgian Lace
Belgian Linen
Belgian Waffle
Believe In Magic
Believe It Or Not
Bellamy
Bellwether
Belogorsky
Beluga
Belvedere
Be Mine
Be My Guest
Be My Valentine
Benchmark
Benediction
Benefactor
Benefit Of The Doubt
Benefit's Package
Bennington
Bentley
Beowulf
Be Realistic
Beringer

*Photo contributed by Darrell Dodds, American Paint Horse
Association and the Paint Horse Journal of Fort Worth, TX.*

Berkeley
Berkshire
Bermuda Triangle
Bernoulli's Principle
Be Specific
Best Behavior
Best Believe It
Best Bet
Best Bluff
Best Brand
Best Buddy
Best By Far
Best Caliber
Best Chance
Best Communication
Best Deception
Best Ever
Best Evidence
Best Example
Best Friend
Best Guess
Best Intentions
Best Judgment
Best Kept Secret
Best Laid Plans

Best Man
Best Mistake
Best Of All
Best Of Everything
Best Offer
Best Of Luck
Best Of The Best
Best Of Times
Best Part
Best Rating
Best Regards
Best Seller
Best Shot
Best Smile
Best Wishes
Best Yet
Beta Rhythms
Bethesda
Better Days
Better Half
Better Judgment
Better Odds
Better Than Ever
Better Than The Boys
Better Things To Do

Between Jobs
Between The Lines
Bet Your Life
Bet Your Money
Bet You Will
Beverly Hills
Bewitched
Bewitching Hour
Bianchi
Bide Your Time
Bien Entendu
Bienvenue
Big Spender
Bijou
Bikini Atoll
Billings
Bill Of Rights
Biloxi
Biorhythms
Birmingham
Bisbee
Biscotti
Bismarck
Bite The Bullet
Bittersweet

Bituminous
Bixby
Blackboard Jungle
Blacksmith
Blade Runner
Blame It On Rio
Blanc Nugae
Blank Check
Blank Page
Blarney Stone
Blasé
Blasphemy
Blazer
Blazing Star
Bless The Stars
Blind Ambition
Blind Date
Blind Faith
Blind Fate
Blind Luck
Blindman's Bluff
Blind Trust
Blink Of An Eye
Blintzes
Blissful

Blizzard
Blockbuster
Block Party
Blow Me A Kiss
Blur
Blustery Day
Blythe Spirit
B.M.O.C.
Board Member
Bodacious
Bo Diddley
Body Language
Body Of Evidence
Bogus
Bohemian
Bolero
Bonafide
Bon Ami
Bonanza
Bonaparte
Bon Appetite
Bon Bon
Bonifide Image
Bonifide Offer
Bonjour

Bonjour Monsieur
Bonjourno
Bonsai
Bon Soir
Bontemps
Bonton
Bonus
Bonus Buy
Bonus Plan
Bonus Point
Bon Voyage
Boogie
Boogie On Down
Boogie Woogie
Bookworm
Booming Business
Boot Camp
Boot Hill Memory
Bordeaux
Bordelaise
Borderline
Bordertown
Born Again
Born To Be Happy
Born Yesterday

Boston Tea Party
Botticelli
Bottom Line
Bougainvillea
Boulevard
Bounce
Bounce Back
Bound By Honor
Bound For Glory
Bound For Hollywood
Bound To Please
Bounty Hunter
Bouquet
Bourbon
Boutique
Brahms
Brahm's Lullaby
Brain Wave
Brand New
Brand X
Brandy
Brandywine
Brass Ring
Brass Tacks
Bravado

Braveheart
Bravissimo
Bravo
Brazen
Breach Of Contract
Breach Of Promise
Break Dance
Breaking Away
Breaking Tradition
Breakout
Break The Ice
Break The Law
Break The Rules
Breakthrough
Breath Of Fresh Air
Breath Of Scandal
Breath Of Spring
Breath Taking
Brevity
Brewster
Brewster's Million
Bric A Brac
Brideshead
Brief Encounter
Brigadier General

Brigadoon
Bright Edge
Bright Eyes
Bright Idea
Bright Lights
Bright Prospect
Bright Spot
Bright Tomorrows
Brilliant Observation
Brilliant Ovation
Brilliantissima

Bring In The
    Reinforcements
Bring Out The Best
Broad Brush
Broadway
Broadcast News
Broadway Blues
Broadway Bound
Broadway Debut
Broadway Limited

Broadway News
Bronx Cheer
Bronze Beauty
Bronze Leaf
Brotherly Love
Brouhaha
Brouwer's Beauty
Brownstone
Bubbling Brown
    Sugar
Bucephalus
Buchanan
Buckingham Palace
Budding Beauty
Budding Chance
Buena Vista
Buffalo Wings
Bugle Player
Buick
Built To Last
Bulletproof
Bullwinkle
Burbank
Burden Of Proof
Bureaucrat

Burgundy
Burgundy Glow
Buried Treasure
Burlington
Business As Usual
Business Casual
Business Partner
Business Plan
Busy Signal
Butch Cassidy
Butterfield Eight
Butterfly Kiss
Buttermilk
Butter Rum
Butterscotch Sundae
Buzz Word
By A Landslide
By All Means
By Appointment Only
By Candlelight
By Default
By Design
Bye Bye Birdie
By Gershwin
By Invitation

Bloody Mary is named for her fleabitten-gray color (a gray horse flecked with red hairs.) Photo contributed by Nanci Falley, American Indian Horse Registry of Lockhart, TX. Nanci mentions the color can also be called bloodsweating gray.

Bylaw
By Moonlight
By Osmosis
By Prescription
By Proxy
By Request
By Scientific
   Standards
By Special Request
By The Book
By The By
By The Clock
By The Minute
By The Rules
By The Way
By Way Of
Byzantine

C

Cabaret
Cabernet
Cabin Fever
Cadbury

Caddy Shack
Cadence Caper
Cadenza
Cadillac
Caesar
Café Au Lait
Cafe Noir
Cafe Society
Caffeine Free
Cagney
Caine Mutiny
Cakewalk
Calculated Risk
Calculating
Calculus
Calico Sky
California Caviar
California Dreaming
California Poppy
California Raisin
California Sky
Call Collect
Call For Action
Calligraphy
Calling Card

Call Me In The
   Morning
Call Me Lately
Call My Bluff
Call Of Duty
Call To Action
Call To Destiny
Call To Duty
Call Waiting
Call To Arms
Calvin Klein
Calypso
Cake Walk
Cambridge
Camden
Camden Yards
Camelot
Camembert
Cameo
Cameo Appearance
Camera Bug
Camera Ready
Camera Shy
Campaign Chairman
Camp Counselor

Camptown Racer
Canadian Club
Canasta
Can Can
Candelabra
Candle In The Dark
Can Do
Candor
Canned Heat
Can't Be Beat
Canterbury Tales
Caper
Cape Town
Capital Express
Capital Gains
Capitol Hill
Cappuccino
Capricious
Captain
Captain Marvel
Captain Marvelous
Captain Planet
Captain's Treasure
Captain Video
Captivated

Captivating
Captive Audience
Capture The Moment
Carbonated
Card-Carrying
   Member
Cardigan
Cardinal Rule
Card Shark
Career Counselor
Career Move
Career Change
Career Path
Carefree
Careless Talk
Care Package
Caricature
Carlisle
Carnival
Carnival Time
Carolina Blues
Carousel
Carpe Diem
Carpetbagger
Carrington

Carry Me Back
Carry Me Over
Carte Blanche
Cartier
Caruso
Carved In Stone
Casablanca
Casbah
Case Closed
Case Dismissed
Case In Point
Case Study
Caseworker
Cash Demand
Cash Flow
Cash McCall
Cashmere
Cash Up Front
Casino
Casino Royal
Casper
Caspian Sea
Cassidy
Cassis
Cassius

Cast A Spell
Castaway
Cast In Stone
Cast Of Characters
Casual Acquaintance
Casual Affair
Casual Connection
Casual Day
Casual Observer
Cause Of Action
Catalina Island
Catalytic Action
Catalytic Converter
Catatonic State
Catch 22
Catch A Dream
Catch A Flight
Catch As Catch Can
Catch Attention
Catch A Wave
Catch Hell
Catch My Drift
Catch Some Air
Catch The Glow
Catch The Magic

Catch The Spirit
Catch The Vibes
Catchy Logo
Catchy Tune
Cat In The Hat
Cat Of Nine Tails
Cat's Cradle
Cat's Meow
Caught In A Spell
Caught In The Act
Cauliflower
Cause For
   Celebration
Causing A
   Commotion
Cavalier
Caveat
Caviar
C.C.
C.C. Ryder
Celebration
Celebration Station
Celebrity
Celebrity Guest
Celestial Empire

Celestial Influence
Celestial Season
Center Court
Centerfield
Centerfold
Center Of Attention
Center Of The
   Universe
Center Stage
Central Casting
Central Park
C.E.O.
Certainly
C'est Bon
C'est La Vie
C'est Moi
Chablis
Cha Cha
Chadbourne
Chadwick
Chain Of Command
Chain Reaction
Chairman Of
   The Board
Challenger

Chamber Music
Chambray
Chamois
Chamomile
Champion
Champs Elysses
Chance Encounter
Chance Of A Lifetime
Chance Of Rain
Chance Of Showers
Chances Are
Chandler
Chanel
Change In Plans
Changemaker
Change Of Heart
Change Of Name
Change Of Pace
Change Of Plans
Changing Conditions
Changing Times
Changing Weather
Channel Surfer
Chanticleer
Chapel Bells

Chapter Eleven
Chapter Two
Character Actor
Character Witness
Charade
Chardonnay
Charge Account
Charge Card
Charge It
Charge My Account
Chariot Of Fire
Charisma
Charity
Charlemagne
Charleston
Charmed Life
Chartered Airways
Charter Member
Chase The Blues
Chase The Moon
Chase The Wind
Chasing Moonbeams
Chasing Rainbows
Chasing Shadows
Chatham

Chattanoochie
Chatterbox
Chaucer
Cheap Thrill
Cheat Notes
Checkers
Checking Account
Check In Time
Check It Out
Checkmate
Cheek To Cheek
Cheeky
Cheerios
Cheer Me On
Cheers
Cheesecake
Chemical Equation
Chemical Reaction
Chenille
Cherished One
Cherish The Moment
Cherry Blossom
Chesapeake
Cheshire Cat
Chessmaster

Chester
Chesterfield
Chestershire
Chesterton
Chest Of Jewels
Cheval
Chianti
Chicken Soup
Chicklet
Chickory
Chief Advisor
Chief Executive
Chief Honcho
Chief Inspector
Chief Justice
Chief Of Protocol
Chief Of Staff
Chief Petty Officer
Chili Con Carne
Chili Verde
Chill Out
Chilled Wine
Chimichanga
Chimney Sweep
China Beach

China Moon
China Town
Chinook Wind
Chips Ahoy
Chit Chat
Chivalry In Action
Chivas Regal
Choctaw
Choice Property
Chorizo
Chortle
Chosen Few
Christmas Angel
Christmas Bonus
Christmas Past
Christmas Spirit
Chutney
C.I.A.
Ciao
Cincinnati
Cinnabar
Cinnamon
Cinnamon Hill
Cinnamon Stick
Circles In The Sand

Circuit Breaker
Circuit Judge
Circumstantial
  Evidence
Citadel
Citizen Kane
City Banker
City Lights
City Limits
City Of Light
City Planner
City Silence
City Slicker
City Sporter
City Suit
Civil Liberty
Claim To Fame
Clairvoyant
Clandestine Meeting
Claret
Class Act
Class Action
Class Clown
Class Honors
Classical Tune

Classic Cut
Classic Edition
Classic Impression
Classic Lines
Classic Look
Classic Performance
Classified Info
Classmate
Class President
Class Promotion
Clean Cut
Clean Slate
Clean Sweep
Clear As A Bell
Clear Cut
Clear Frontier
Clear Horizons
Clear Illusions
Clearing Skies
Clearly Canadian
Clearly Crystal
Clearly Dutch
Clearly First
Clearly Number One
Clearly Royal

Clear Sailing
Clear The Air
Clear The Way
Clearwater
Cleopatra
Clever Appointment
Clever Endeavor
Clever Trick
Cleverly Concealed
Cliché
Cliffs Of Dover
Climbing Interest
Clinging Vine
Clinical Psychologist
Clippership
Clock Watcher
Clone
Closed Circuit
Close Encounter
Close Enough
Close To None
Close-Up
Close Watch
Closing Argument
Closing The Ring

Closing Time
Clothes Horse
Clover Leaf
Clue
Clueless
Coast Is Clear
Coast To Coast
Coat Of Arms
Cobbler
Cockamamie
Cocky
Cocoa Butter
Code Of Ethics
Code Of Excellence
Code Of Honor
Coffee Break
Cognac
Coin Of The Realm
Coin Operated
Coke Classic
Cold Shoulder
Collage
Collect All
Collective Bargaining
Collective Soul

Collector's Item
College Bound
College Grad
College Tuition
Colorado Springs
Colossal Gains
Come Monday
Come September
Comet
Comfort Zone
Comic Relief
Comic Strip
Coming Attraction
Coming Of Age
Coming Up Roses
Commander In Chief
Commanding
 Presence
Command
 Performance
Comme Ci,
 Comme Ca
Commisioned Officer
Common
 Denominator

Common Ground
Common Knowledge
Common Law
Common Practice
Common Sense
Commotion
Communications
 Expert
Compadre
Company Man
Company Manners
Company Policy
Compassionate One
Compelling
Competitive Edge
Complete Surrender
Composite Drawing
Compound Interest
Compton
Compulsion
Compulsive
Compulsive Flyer
Compulsive Gambler
Computer Chip
Computer Literate

Top left: Geronimo and Cecily Powers.
Photo contributed by Trudy Powers of Sebastopol, CA.
Bottom left: Sebastian and Kim Citelli.
Photo contributed by Kim Citelli of Goshen, NY.
Above: 32-year-old Bucky and Linda Yount. Photo
contributed by Suzanne Drnec of Chino, CA.

Comrade In Arms
Con Artist
Concentration
Concerned Citizen
Concerted Effort
Concerto In B Minor
Conditioned
    Response
Conscientious
Conclusive
Conclusive Evidence
Conclusive Proof
Condition Of
    Anonymity
Conducive
Conestoga
Confederate
Conference Call
Confidant
Confucius Say
Congressional Action
Conjunction
Conquest
Conscientious
    Objector

Considerate
Conspicuous
Conspiracy
Conspiracy Theory
Conspirator
Constant Chatter
Constant Comment
Constant
    Commentary
Constant Companion
Constant Reminder
Constitution
Constitutional
    Amendment
Contender
Contest Winner
Continuity
Continuous Applause
Contraband
Contradiction
Contradiction In Terms
Contributing Editor
Controversy
Conundrum
Conventional Wisdom

Conversation Piece
Conversion
Conviction
Convinced
Copacabana
Co-Pilot
Coping
Copy Cat
Copy Editor
Copyright
Copyright Invasion
Coquette
Cordially Yours
Corduroy
Coriander
Corner Cop
Corner The Market
Cornucopia
Corporate Executive
Corona
Correction
Cosmic Energy
Cosmic Force
Cosmo
Cosmopolitan

Cosmopolitan
    Gentleman
Costly Jewel
Cotillion
Countdown
Counter Balance
Counter Offer
Counterpart
Counterpoint
Count Me In
Count My Blessings
Count On Me
Country Fair
Country Fest
Country Music
Country Path
Country Road
Country Swing
County Line
Count Your Blessings
Coup De Grace
Coupe D'Etat
Coupe DeVille
Courageous
Course Of Action

Court Appeal
Courtesy Call
Court Jester
Court Of Appeals
Court Order
Court Ruling
Courvoiser
Cover Story
Covert
Cover-Up
Coveted
Coworker
C.P.A.
Cracked Ice
Cracker Jack
Craftsman
Cranberry
Cranberry Days
Cranberry Ice
Cream Of Tartar
Cream Of The Crop
Cream Sherry
Creative Intentions
Creative Moves
Creative Outlet

Credit Risk
Creek's Rising
Creme De La Creme
Crescendo
Crescent Moon
Cricket
Crimes Of The Heart
Crimestopper
Criterion
Critical Choice
Critical Decision
Critical Mass
Critical Moment
Critical Path
Critical Thinker
Critic's Choice
Crossing Zone
Cross My Heart
Cross The Line
Crowd Pleaser
Crown Colony
Crown Jewel
Crowning Glory
Cruise Control
Cruiseliner

Cruiser
Cruising High
Crusader
Crushed Velvet
Cry Freedom
Crystal Ball
Crystal Clear
Crystal Vision
Cry Wolf
Cucaracha
Culligan Man
Culture Clash
Culture Shock
Cumberland
Curfew
Curiosity
Curmudgeon
Current Affairs
Current Event
Curtain Call
Custom Caddy
Custom Finery
Customer Service Rep
Custom Made
Cut A Deal

Cut Loose
Cutting Edge
Cutting It Close
Cut To The Chase
Cutty Sark
Cutting Taxes
Cybernetix
Cyberspace
Cygnet
Cypress Gardens
Cyprus
Cyrano

Darwin's Theory
Decision Pending
Dad's Investment
Daffodil
Daggummit
Daily Commute
Daiquiri
Daily Review
Daily Ritual

Dakota
Dakota Highlands
Dalai Lama
Dalliance
Dance Fever
Dance Master
Dance Sequence
Dancing In The Street
Dancing On Air
Dancing Twilight
Dancin' On The
  Boulevard
Daredevil
Dash For Cash
Dashing Ways
Dare To Be Different
Dare To Be There
Dare To Dream
Dash Of Flair
Database
Dauntless
Davenport
Daybreak
Daydream Believer
Daydreamer

Daydreams
Day Glow
Day In Court
Day In, Day Out
Day Job
Days Like These
Day's Work
Daytime Drama
Daytime Magic
Daytime Soaps
Dazzled
D-Day
Dealer's Choice
Dealer's Delight
Deal Me In
Dean's List
Dear Diary
Debonair
Debut
Decadence
Decadent Dessert
Decatur
Decidedly Irish
Decipher
Decisive

Declaring Bankruptcy
Deck The Halls
Decoration
Découpage
Decoy
Dedication
Deep Water
Defensive Mover
Deficit Spending
Definitive Plan
Defying Gravity
Deja Vu
Delaney
De Lorean
Demanding Market
Democracy Reigns
Denmark
Delancey Street
Delicate Touch
Delightful
Deliverance
Deliver The Goods
Deluxe Model
De Mille
Departure Time

Dependability
Dependable
Desert Fox
Desert Storm
Designated Driver
Designer Label
Designer Genes
Designer Jeans
Designer's Sample
Desktop Publisher
Des Moines
Desoto
Desperado
Dessert Menu
Destination Anywhere
Destiny
Destiny Calls
Destiny's Guest
Detail Oriented
Detected
Détente
Detention Hall
Determined Destiny
Detroit Disciple
Detroit's Piston

Detour
Dewey
Dew Drop
Diablo
Dialing For Dollars
Diamond Back
Diamond Connection
Diamond In The Rough
Diamond Jubilee
Diamond Rio
Diamonds Are Forever
Die Hard
Digital Control
Digital Output
Dilemma
Dilettante
Diligence
Dillingham
Dill Pickel
Dinner For Two
Direct Deposit
Director
Director Of The Board
Director's Chair

Dire Straights
Dirty Dancing
Disclosure
Disco Fever
Discovery Zone
Discretion
Display Of Art
Distinguished Guest
District Attorney
Diversity
Dividends
Divine Order
Dixieland
Dixieland Rhythm
D.N.A.
Doctor John
Doctor's Excuse
Doctor's Orders
Doctor Watson
Documentary
Do Gooder
Doing Business
Doing Time
Domestic Help
Domestic Partner

Dominican
Domino
Domino Theory
Done Deal
Donegal
Donnybrook
Don't Ask Me
Don't Even Ask
Don't Look Back
Don't Rule Me Out
Don't Say Maybe
Don't Tempt Fate
Doonesbury
Door Prize
Door To Door Salesman
Dose Of Reality
Do The Macarena
Do The Math
Double Agent
Double Bogey
Double Call
Double Check
Double Clutch
Double Dare

Doubleday
Double Deal
Double Decker
Double Dutch
Double Entendre
Double Entry
Double Exposure
Double Feature
Double Image
Double Indemnity
Double Meaning
Double Negative
Double-O-Seven
Double-Page Spread
Double Play
Double Portion
Double Risk
Double Space
Double Standard
Double Stuffed
Double Swap
Double Take
Double Talk
Double Vision
Double Whammy

Doubloon
Do Unto Others
Dow Jones
Down Loading
Down The Hatch
Down To Details
Down To Earth
Down To The Wire
Down Under
Dragon Fly
Drama Coach
Drambuie
Drastic Measures
Dream Boat
Dream Catcher
Dream Come True
Dream Field
Dreamin' Out Loud
Dream Interpreter
Dream Machine
Dream Maker
Dream Master
Dream On
Dream Seeker
Dream State

Dream Walkin'
Dream Weaver
Dress For Success
Dress Rehearsal
Driftwood
Driver's Permit
Driving Force
Drizzle
Drop Dead Gorgeous
Drop Of A Hat
Drum Roll Please
Dry Clean Only
Dry Run
Dubious Dialogue
Dublin
Dubonnet
Due North
Due Process
Du Jour
Dulcimer
Duly Noted
Duncan
Dungaree
Duplicate
Duplicater

Duplicate Reaction
Du Printemps
Durable Goods
Duracell
Durango
Du Schon
Dusk 'Til Dark
Dusk To Dawn
Dust Bunny
Dustbuster
Dusty Road
Dutch Courage
Dutch Treat
Duty Bound
Duty Calls
Dylan
Dynasty

Eager Beaver
Eagle Heart
Eagle Scout
Eagle's Flight

Early Bird
Early Bloomer
Early Impression
Early Riser
Earth Angel
Earthshaking News
Easily Amused
Easily Impressed
East Of Eden
East West Express
Easy Does it

Juan Miguel. Photo contributed by the Paso Fino Horse Association of Plant City, FL. Photographer: D. Wohlart.

29

Easy Going
Easy Living
Easy Lovin'
Easy Rider
Easy Street
Easy To Install
Easy To Please
Easy Touch
Ebb Tide
Eccentric
Echo
Echo Of The Past
Eclair
Eclectic
Eclipse
Ecologically Sound
Econoline
Edelweiss
Edge Of Night
Edinburgh
Edsel
Educated Guess
Efficiency Expert
Egghead
Egg Nog

Egocentric
Ego Trip
El Dorado
Elderberry
Elderberry Jammin'
Electorial Vote
Electricity
Electric Light
Electronic Age
Elegance
Eleganté
Elegant Image
Eleventh Hour
Elfin Magic
El Greco
Elite
Ellington
El Paso
Elsewhere
Elusive Butterfly
Elusive Desire
Elusive Dream
Elusive Treason
Embarcadero
Embassy Row

Emblazoned Fool
Embraceable
Emerald City
Emerald Image
Emerald Isle
Emerald Queen
Emerson
Eminent Domain
Emmanuel
E. Motions
Empowered
Empowerment Agent
Empty Bank Account
Emulated
Enchante
Enchanted
Enchanting
Enchantment
Enchilada
Encore
Encounters Of The
    Third Kind
Endless Knot
End Of Story
End Of The Rainbow

Endearment
Endless Possibilities
Energy Expert
English Leather
English Major
English Subtitle
English Toffee
Enigma
Enjoy The Moment
Enjoy The Ride
Enlightened
Enlisted Man
Enough Already
Enough Said
Ensign First Class
Enter Laughing
Enterprising
Entertainer Of
    The Year
Enticing
Enticing Proposition
Entrepreneur
Entropy
Environmental Impact
Envy Me

Enzymatic Action
Enzyme Reaction
Epic
Epstein
Equal Opportunity
Equal Rights
Equilibrium
Equity Earned
Ergo
Erin Go Braugh
Eros
Escalating Plot
Escapade
Escape Artist
Escaped Felon
Escaped From
   Alcatraz
Escape Velocity
Escargot
Escort Service
Esprit
Esprit De Corps
Esquire
Essential
Essential Ingredient

Estimated Time
   Of Arrival
E.T.
E.T.A.
ETC.
Etcetera
Eternal Equinox
Eternally Yours
Eternity
Ethereal
Ethical
Euphrates
Eureka
Eurythmic
Even As We Speak
Even Gamble
Evening Affair
Evening Edition
Evening Journal
Evening Out
Evening Post
Even Kiel
Evergreen
Ever Ready
Ever So Clever

Every Last Dime
Everyman's Fantasy
Evian
Evidence
Evidence For The
   Defense
Evidently So
Evolution
Exact Change
Exacto Mundo
Exactly
Examiner
Example Number One
Excalibur
Excel
Excellent Buy
Exceptionality
Exceptional Taste
Excess Baggage
Exclusive
Exclusive Interview
Exclusive Rights
Excused Absence
Excuse My French
Executive Decision

Executive Material
Executive Order
Executive Priviledge
Exhilaration
Exodus
Exotic Essence
Expeditious
Expendable
Expenditure
Expense Account
Expensive Hand-
   Me-Down
Expertise
Expert System
Expert Witness
Exponential
Express Checkout
Express Delivery
Expression
Expression Of
   Gratitude
Express Yourself
Exquisite
Extended Family
Extended Warranty

Extra Credit
Extra, Extra
Extraordinary
Extra Terrestrial
Extravaganza
Eye Opener
Eye Witness
E.Z. Pickens
E.Z. Ryder

Fable Fantasy
Facade
Facts Are Facts
Facts Are In
Fading Memories
Fahrenheit Rising
Fail Safe
Faint Whisper
Fairbanks
Fair Enough
Fair Exchange
Fairfield

Fair Game
Fairly Breezy
Fairly Certain
Fair Play
Fairwinds
Fait Accompli
Falstaff
Fame's Quest
Familiar Territory
Family Crest
Family Secret
Family Values
Fanatic
Fanciful
Fancy Fixin's
Fancy Free
Fancy That
Fancy This
Fandango
Fanfare
Fanmail
Fantasia
Fantastic
Fantastic Folly
Fantastico

Fantasy
Far Cry
Fare-Thee-Well
Fargo
Far Horizon
Farina
Far More Class
Far Out
Fascinating Rhythm
Fascination
Fashionably Late
Fashion Nugget
Fashion Plate
Fashion Statement
Fast Learner
Fast Pass
Fast Talk
Fast Tract
Fatal Attraction
Fatal Beauty
Fatalist
Fat Chance
Fat City
Fate
Fatty McGee

Faux Pas
Favorable Sign
Favorite Charity
Favorite Hobby
Favorite Son
Favorite Subject
Favorite Suspect
Favorite Trick
F.B.I.
Feature Attraction
Feature Film
Feature Story
Feelin' Groovy
Feelings Mutual
Felonious Fable
Fend For Yourself
Feniwink
Fenway
Fessin' Up
Festivity
Few Are Chosen
Few Pointers
Fictitious Character
Fiddler's Corner
Field Day

*Above: Double Take. Photo contributed by
Barbara Mannis of Malvern, PA.
Upper right: Sherry (horse) with, from left, Tara
Thompson, Erin Jacobseon, and Cecily Powers.
Photo contributed by Trudy Powers of Sebastopol, CA.
Lower right: Hartley Adams driven by Leonard
Fleming. Photo contributed by the International
Trottingbred & Pacing Association of Moravia, NY.*

Fielder's Choice
Field Of Dreams
Field Of Vision
Field Trip
Fiesta Time
Fifth Amendment
Fifth Avenue
Fifth Avenue Flair
Fifth Gear
Fifty-One Flavors
Figment Of My
  Imagination
Fig Newton
Figure It Out
Figure Of Speech
Figure Skater
Filegate
Filigree
Filmore
Final Appeal
Final Bid
Final Chapter
Final Copy
Final Countdown
Final Conclusion

Final Curtain
Final Decision
Final Draft
Finale
Final Edition
Final Frontier
Final Judgement
Finally
Finally Finished
Finally Friday
Finally Mine
Final Payment
Final Say
Final Settlement
Final Tribute
Final Word
Final Victim
Finder's Fee
Finders Keepers
Fine Art
Fine China
Fine Detail
Fine Idea
Fine Line
Fine Spirits

Fine Threads
Finer Things
Fine Tune
Fine Wine
Finesse
Finest Caliber
Finest Hour
Finis
Finishing Touch
Finish Line
Finnigan
Firm Believer
Firm Tread
First Amendment
First Appearance
First Assignment
First Audition
First Chance
First Choice
First Citation
First Class
First Crocus
First Day Jitters
First Draft
First Edition

First Honors
First Impression
First In Command
First In Line
First In Flight
First In Line
First Light
First Look
First Love
First Mate
First Mortagage
First Opinion
First Quarter
First Rate
First Release
First Run
First Things First
First Thought
First Union
Fit As A Fiddle
Fit For A King
Fit Of Fury
Fit To A Tee
Fit To Be Tied
Fit To Print

Fitzgerald
Five Easy Pieces
Five-Star Rating
Flair
Flash Dancer
Flash Flood
Flash In The Pan
Flawless
Flea Market Treasure
Fleeting Fame
Fleeting Glance
Fleeting Moment
Fleet Street
Fleetwood
Flew The Coop
Flightmaster
Flight Of Fancy
Flight Of Fantasy
Flight Of Ideas
Flight Time
Flighty Flyer
Flintlock
Flintstone
Flirtatious
Floppy Disc

Flower Drum Song
Flowmaster
Fly By Night
Fly First Class
Fly Free
Flyhawk
Flying Carpet
Flying Cloud
Flying Dutchman
Flying Encounters
Flying Fedora
Flying Font
Flying High
Flying Saucer
Flying Swan
Flying Tiger
Fly Me To Rio
Fly Me To The Moon
Focal Point
Focus
Focus Of Attention
Foggy Bottom
Follow The Leader
Fond Farewell
Food For Thought

Foolish Pursuit
Foolish Question
Foolproof
Footnote
For A Change
For Any Occasion
For Appearance's
    Sake
For A Song
Forbidden Fruit
Forbidden Treasure
Force Of Habit
Force Of One
Forecast
Forced Entry
Foregone Conclusion
Foreign Affairs
Foreign
    Correspondent
Foreign Dignitary
Foreign Exchange
Foreign Influence
Foreign Legacy
Foreign Traveler
Forerunner

Forest Hills
Forever And Ever
Forever Faithful
Forever Young
Forever Yours
Forewarned
Forget Me Not
Forget Paris
Forgotten Promise
For Heaven's Sake
For Keeps
Formality
Formal Protest
For Members Only
Formosa
For Old Time Sake
For Real
For Sure
For The Good Times
For The Moment
For The Record
Fortitude
Fortune 500
Fortune Hunter
Fortune Teller

Forty Niner
Forty Winks
Forty-Year Dream
Founding Father
Found Innocent
Found My Niche
Four Leaf Clover
Four Of A Kind
Four On The Floor
Four Runner
Four Seasons
Four Square
Fourteen Carat
Fourth Dimension
Four-Wheel Drive
Foxtrot
Fragile
Frame Of Reference
Framework
Frankly Awesome
Free Account
Free Agent
Free As The Wind
Freedom Fighter
Freedom Hall

Freedom Of Speech
Freedom Rider
Freedom Rings
Freelance
Free Style
Freestyle
Freetime
Freeway Speed
Freeze Frame
French Connection
French Coup
French Pastry
French Silk
French Twist
Frequent Flyer
Fresh Approach
Fresh Start
Fried Green
    Tomatoes
Friendly Gesture
Friendly Persuasion
Fringe Benefit
Frivolous
From One Extreme
From The Heart

Front And Center
Frontline Phenomena
Front Man
Front Money
Front Page
Front Page News
Front Page Story
Front Row Seat
Front Runner
Full Back
Full Circle
Full Clip
Full Cry
Fullerton
Full Figured
Full Force
Full House
Full Monty
Full Moon
Full Moon Rising
Full Of Adventure
Full Of Enterprise
Full Of Fun
Full Page Ad
Full Sail

Full Scale
Full Tilt
Funnybone
Funny Money
Funny Pages
Funny Valentine
Future Forecast
Future Shock
Fuzzy Logic
F.Y.I.

Gabardine
Gabriel
Gaining Altitude
Gait Master
Gala
Galapagos
Galaxy
Gallagher
Gallant One
Galliano
Galloping Gourmet

Galloway
Gallup Poll
Gambit
Gambler's Choice
Game Day
Game Plan
Games People Play
Game Winner
Garden Variety
Garrison
Geeky
Gee Whiz
Gekko
Gemstone
Gender Bender
Gene Pool
General Delivery
General Impression
General Practitioner
General Public
General Staff
Generation Gap
Generation X
Genesis
Gentle Rogue

Genuflect
Genuine Article
Genuine Facts
German Mark
Gestalt
Get A Clue
Get A Job
Get A Life
Get On With It
Get Real
Get Rich Quick
Get Serious
Get Shorty
Get Smart
Get The Drift
Get The Fax
Get The Message
Get The Picture
Get The Point
Ghiradelli Square
Gibraltar
Gideon
Gifted
Gift Horse
Gift Of Gab

Gift Wrapped
Gingham
Ginseng
Giovanni
Gitano
Give A Hoot
Give Me A Break
Give Me Five
Give Me Liberty
Give Me The Works
Gizmo
Glad Hand
Glad Tidings
Gladstone
Glamorous
Glass Slipper
Gleeful
Glimmerick
Glimmer Of Hope
Glitch
Glitterman
Global Influence
Global Warming
Globetrotter
Glorious

G.N.P.
Goal Keeper
Goal Tender
Goal Post
Godsend
Godspeed
Go Dutch
Go For Broke
Go For It
Go Forth
Go Getter
Going My Way
Going Overboard
Going Places
Going To Extremes
Gone Hollywood
Gone Public
Gone To Lunch
Gone With The Wind
Good Catch
Good Chance
Good Chemistry
Good Company
Good Deed
Good Fortune

Shire. Photo contributed by Trudy Powers of Sebastopol, CA.

Good Friday
Good Gracious
Good Hair Day
Good Humor
Good Intentions
Good Luck Charm
Good Measure
Goodness Gracious
Good News
Good Old Days
Good Samaritan
Good Sport

Good Stuff
Good Time Charlie
Good Times
Good Vibrations
Good Year Blimp
Gordian Knot
Gossamer
Gossamer Wings
Gossamer Veil
Gotcha
Got Charisma
Go The Distance
Got The Green Light
Got My Wish
Go To The Source
Go To Town
Got Religion
Got To Be
Gourmet Style
Gourmet Treat
Government Worker
Go With The Flow
Graceful
Grace Period
Gracious

Grade A
Grade Point Average
Grafitti
Grammy Nominee
Granola Bar
Grant A Pardon
Graphic Designer
Grass Hopper
Gratitude
Gratuity
Great Adventure
Great Bend
Great Escape
Great Expectations
Great Gumption
Great Imposter
Great Persuasion
Great Pretender
Green Beret
Green Card
Greenpeace
Greensleeves
Green With Envy
Groovy
Ground Cover

Growing Concern
Guacamole
Guaranteed Fresh
Guardian Angel
Gucci
Guess Again
Guesstimate
Guess What?
Guess Who?
Guesswork
Guest Of Honor
Guest Speaker
Guidance Counselor
Guiding Light
Guilt By Association
Guilt-Free
Guilt Ridden
Guilty As Charged
Guilty As Sin
Guilty Secret
Guinness
Gullible
Gumption
Gumshoe
Gun Shy

Gung Ho
Guns Ablazing
Gunther
Guru
Gust Of Wind
Gypsy
Gypsy Dancer

H20
Häagen Dazs
Haber Dasher
Hail To The Chief
Halcyon Days
Hale Bop
Haley's Comet
Half A Chance
Hallelujah
Hallmark
Hall Of Fame
Hall Of Justice
Hallowed Halls
Hall Pass

Halston
Hamilton
Hampton
Hand Jive
Handle With Care
Handmade
Hand Of Fate
Handsome Reward
Hang Time
Hanson
Happenstance
Happily Ever After
Happy Camper
Happy Days
Happy Ending
Happy Go Lucky
Happy Hour
Happy Landing
Happy Medium
Happy Returns
Happy To Be Me
Happy Trails
Harbor Light
Harmonium
Harrigan

Harvard Lawyer
Harvest Moon
Hassle Free
Hasta La Vista
Haste Makes Waste
Hat Trick
Hats Off
Hav-A-Java
Havana
Have No Shame
Haversham
Have You Heard
Hawkeye
Hawthorne
Hay Dude
Head For The Hills
Head Honcho
Headhunter
Headline Story
Headliner
Head Of The Class
Head Over Heels
Headspin
Head Turner
Heard The News

Hear Me Out
Hear My Plea
Hearsay
Heartbreaker
Heartlight
Heart Of Hearts
Hearts Are Trump
Heart's Delight
Heart's Desire
Heartstring
Heartthrob
Heart To Heart
Heat Of The Knight
Heaven Can Wait
Heaven Help Us
Heaven Only Knows
Heaven Sent
Heavy Metal
Heebee Geebees
Heidelburg
Heinrich
Heintz
Heirloom
Heir To The Throne
Helium

Hellion's Wrath
Hello Gorgeous
Helping Hand
Helter Skelter
Hennessey
Henry's Model "A"
Henry The VIII
Here Comes The Judge
Here's Lookin' At You
Heresy
Here To Eternity
Here To Stay
Heritage
Hermes
Hero's Image
Hero Worship
Herringbone
Hibiscus
Hidden Agenda
Hidden Asset
Hidden Clause
Hidden Delight
Hidden Talent
Hidden Treasure

Hideaway
Highway Patrol
Hillbilly Heaven
Hill Street Blues
Hint Of Heaven
Hint Of Mint
Hint Of Scandal
Hip Hip Hurrah
Hip Mama
Hippocrates
Hippocratic Oath
History Buff
Hitherto
Hit Parade
Hit The Deck
Hit Tune
Ho Hum
Hobgoblin
Hobo
Hockey Jock
Hocus Pocus
Hoffman
Hogan's Hero
Hold Harmless
Hold That Thought

Hold The Dream
Hold The Mayo
Hold Your Applause
Hold Your Own
Hole In One
Holiday Blues
Holiday Spirit
Hollingsworth
Holllywood
Hollywood Hoopla
Hombre
Home Brew
Home By Dark
Home Free
Home On The Range
Home Remedy
Home Run
Hometown Favorite
Hometown Hero
Homeward Bound
Homework
Honorable Mention
Honor Bound
Honor Bright
Honor Student

Honor Roll
Honor System
Hope Springs Eternal
Hopscotch
Horoscope
Horsefeathers
Hot Commodity
Hot Cross Buns
Hot Days
Hot Licks
Hotline
Hot Off The Press
Hot Pepper
Hotpoint
Hot Property
Hot Pursuit
Hot Rod
Hottentott
Hot Tip
Hot Toddy
Hot Topic
Houlihan
Hour Of Need
House Account
House Of Cards

House Rules
Houston
How Sweet It Is
Hulabaloo
Humanitarian
Humdinger
Hummer
Hung Jury
Hunkey-Dory
Huntington
Hurricane
Hushabye
Hush Puppy
Hyde Park
Hydroplane
Hypnotic Trance
Hypnotized
Hypotenuse
Hypothetically
    Speaking

I

I Believe In Magic
I Believe In Miracles
Icebreaker
Ice Cream Sundae
Icon
Iconoclastic
Ideal
Idealistic
Idealize
Ideal World
Ideology
Ides Of March
Idiom
Idiosyncrasy
Idle Chatter
Idle Gossip
Idle Speculation
Idle Talk
Idle Times
Idle Ways
I Do Declare

I Don't Think So
I Dream Of Genie
Ignition
I Just Wanna Fly
I Like Ike
I'll Be Darned
Ill-Gotten Gains
Illuminated
Illusion
Illusions Of Grandeur
Illusive
Illusive Butterfly
Illustrious
Illustrious Leader
I'm A Believer
Imagemaker
Imaginary Friend
Imagination
Imagine That
I'm Innocent
Imitator
Immeasurable
Immediacy
Immediately
Immediate Infusion

Immediate
    Occupancy
Immortal
Impala
Impartial
Impatient
Impeccable
Impeccable
    Credentials
Impeccable Taste
Imperial Design
Imperial Guard
Impertinent
Impossible Dream
Impressionable
Impressions
Impressive
Impressive Blend
Impressive Gift
Impromptu
Impulsive
I'm Tiger Woods
In 3-D
In A Different League
In A Flash

41

In A Heartbeat
In A Niche
In Another World
In A Pinch
In Arrears
In A Trance
In Bounds
In Cahoots
Incandescent
Incantation
Incentive Plan
Incidental
In Clover
Incognito
In Command
Incomparable
In Concert
In Conclusion
Inconclusive
Inconspicuous
In Costume
Incredible
Incumbent Candidate
In Custody
In Debt

In Demand
In Denial
Independence Day
Independencia
Independently
    Wealthy
In Depth Review
Indicted
Indiscreet
Indispensable
Individuality
Indivisible
Indubitably
Inducement
Industrious
Industry Standard
Indy 500
In Essence
Inevitable
Inevitable Outcome
In Excess
Infatuation
Infinite Wisdom
Infinity
Influential

In Focus
Informed Consent
In Gear
In Good Taste
In Harmony
In Harm's Way
Inheritance
Inherit The Wind
In High Regard
In Honor Of
Initial Link
In Left Field
In My Court
In My Heyday
In My Own Image
In My Prime
Inner Circle
Innocent Bystander
Innovation
Innovative
Innuendo
In Orbit
In Overdrive
In Overtime
In Plain Sight

In Plain View
In Question
Inquire Within
Inquisitive
In Reality
In Real Life
In Recovery
In Retrospect
In Rhythm
In Sheep's Clothing
In Short Supply
Inside Edge
Inside Moves
Insider Trading
Inside Straight
Inside Track
Insight
Insomnia
Insomniac
Inspiration
Inspiration Point
Inspired
Installment Plan
Instant Rapport
Instant Remedy

Instant Replay
In Stereo
In Style
In Summary
In Suspense
In Sync
In Tandem
Integrity
Interception
Interest Free
Interlude
Internal Affairs
Internet Update
In The Abstract
In The Affirmative
In The Beginning
In The Blink Of An Eye
In The Fast Lane
In The Fast Track
In The Floodlights
In The Fold
In The Footlights
In The Forefront
In The Groove

In The Habit
In The Key Of "Gee"
In The Know
In The Limelight
In The Line Of Duty
In The Majors
In The Mob
In The Mood
In The News
In Theory
In The Pink
In The Public Eye
In The Right Direction
In The Spotlight
In The Swing Of Things
In The Tradition
In The White House
In The Zone
Into Mischief
Into Oblivion
Into The Breech
Into The Future
Into The Storm
Intoxicated
Intrepid Hero

Intrepidity
Intrepid Thinker
Intrepid Thunder
Intrigue
Intrigued
Introspective
Intuition
Intuitive
In Unison
Invasion Of Privacy
Invest A Mint
Investigative Reports
Investigator
Investment In Time
Investment Property
Investor's Market
Investor's Trust
Invincible
Invisible Ink
Invisible Playmate
In Vogue
In Your Dreams
In Your Honor
In Your Wildest Dreams

In X. S.
Iowa
Ipso Facto
I Rest My Case
Irish Cream
Irish Coffee
Irish Eyes "R" Smiling
Irish Linen
Irish Mist
Irish Pride
Irish Toffee
Irksome
Ironclad Alibi
Iron Eagle
Iron Glove
Iron In The Fire
Ironsides
Irreplaceable
Irresistible
Irresistible Force
I.R.S.
I.R.S. Refund
Ishkabibble
Island Time

43

"Isle" Be Cool
Isosceles
Isosceles Dilemna
I Spy
Itemized Deduction
It Figures
It's About Time
It's A Crazy Life
It's A Given
It's A Mind Game
It's Greek To Me
It's It
I've got Rhythm
Ivy League
I was Framed

J

Jacuzzi
Jaguar
Jailbait
Jalapeño
Jalopy
Jamaica

Jamboree
Jammin'
Jam Session
January Moon
Japonica
Jargon
Jasmine
Jaunty Jester
Java Beans
Jazz Standard
Jeepers Peepers
Jenerio
Jester's Joke
Jet Lag
Jet Set
Jetsetter
Jet Stream
Jeweler's Row
Jigsaw
Jigsaw Puzzle
Jingle All The Way
Jitterbug
Jog Your Memory
Johnny Jump-Up
Joie De Vivre

Joint Enterprise
Joint Forces
Join The Force
Joint Venture
Joker's Wild
Jolly Good
Jolly Jonquil
Jollywell Might
Jordache
Joshua Tree
Jot It Down
Journal Entry
Journey
Journeyman
Journey's End
Joyful
Joyful Occasion
Joyful Revenge
Joy Rider
Jubilant
Jubilation
Jubilee
Judgement Call
Judgement Day
Juggernaught

Juicy Scoop
Ju-Jit-Sue
Jumped Bail
Jump For Joy
Jumping Junipers
Jumpshot
Jump Start
Jump The Gun
Jump To Conclusions
Jungle Vibes
Juniper
Junk Bond
Jupiter
Jurassic Park
Juris Prudence
Jury Foreman
Jury Member
Jury Duty
Jury's Out
Jus' Jivin'
Just A Bargain
Just A Blur
Just A Breeze
Just About Perfect
Just Add Water

Just A Flirt
Just A Formality
Just A Gigolo
Just A Hunch
Just Another Day
Just A Power Play
Just A Reminder
Just Arrived
Just A Rumor
Just A Saint
Just A Show Off
Just Ask Me
Just Because
Just Before Dark
Just Beginning
Just Between Us
Just Compensation
Just Cruisin'
Just Desserts
Just Exceptional
Just For Fun
Just For Starters
Just Friends
Just Happened
Just Humor Me

Justice For All
Justice Due
Justice League
Justice Of The Peace
Justice Served
Just Imagine
Just In Case
Just Incredible
Just In Thyme
Just In Time
Just Joking
Just Kidding
Just Like Magic
Just My Imagination
Just My Luck
Just My Style
Just My Type
Just One Look
Just Peachy
Just Perfect
Just Routine
Just Say No
Just Say The Word
Just Say WOW
Just Smile

Just Sue
Just Sue Me
Just Swing Baby
Just The Beginning
Just The Facts
Just The Facts,
  Ma'am
Just Wondering
Juxtaposition

K

Kalamazoo
Kamikaze
Kapow
Karaoke
Karma
Katmandu
Katz Play
Kazoo
K'ching K'ching
Keen
Keen On Me
Keep 'Em Guessing

Keeper Of The Faith
Keeping Notes
Keeping Tabs
Keeping Tempo
Keeping Time
Keeping Up With
  The Joneses
Keep In Touch
Keep Me Posted
Keep My Cool
Keep On Truckin'
Keepsake
Keeps Me Busy
Keeps On Tickin'
Keep The Change
Keep The Faith
Keep The Image
Keep The Magic
Keep The Rhythm
Kemosabe
Kenabec
Keno
Kensington
Kentucky Blue Grass
Kentucky Sky

45

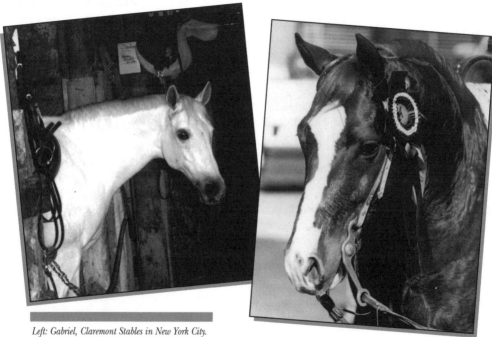

Left: Gabriel, Claremont Stables in New York City.
Right: Smartin' Off. Both photos contributed by
Suzanne Drnec of Chino, CA.

Keogh Plan
Kept My Promise
Kerry
Key Biscayne
Key Decision Maker
Key Largo
Keynote Speaker
Key Player
Key Signature
Keys To My Heart
Keystone
Keystone Cop
Keys To The City
Key To Success
Key To The Mint
Key West
Key Witness
Khaki
Kibitz
Kibosh
Kilimanjaro
Killarney
Killing Time
Kind Hearted
Kindred Spirit

Kinetic Theory
Kingdom Come
King's Ransom
Kingston
Kipling
Kismet
Kittyhawk
Kiwi
Klondike
Knickerbocker
Knock On Wood
Knowledge Is Power
Know The Ropes
Kodak Moment
Kopy Kat
Korbel
Kruggarand
Kryptonite

L

Labor Intensive
Labor Of Love
Labor Saving Device

L.A. Clipper
La Costa
La-De-Da
La Difference
L.A. Dodger
Lafayette
L.A. Gear
Lagerfeld
L.A. Laker
LaLa Palooza
Lalique
Lamborghini
Lancer
Landcruiser
Landlover
Landmark Case
Landmark Decision
Land Of Opportunity
Landowner
Landrover
Landsakes
Landscaper
Land's End
Landslide
Langford

Lansing
L.A.P.D.
Lapse Of Memory
Lap Top
Laredo
Laser Jet
Last Call
Last Chance
Last Dance
Last Detail
Last Exit To Earth
Last Fling
Lasting Impression
Lasting Legacy
Last Laugh
Last Minute Decision
Last Request
Last Shot
Last Stand
Last Stanza
Last Tango
Last Word
Late Arrival
Late Bloomer
Late Breaking News

Latest Discovery
Latest Edition
Latest Fashion
Latest Rumour
Latest Sting
Latest Style
Latin Lingo
Lavender Blue
Lavender Sky
Lawn Ornament
Law Of Nature
Law Of The Land
Lawsuit
Lazy Lifestyle
Lead Crystal
Lead Guitar
Leading Role
Lead Singer
Lead Story
Lean On Me
Leaping Lizard
Leap Of Faith
Leap Year
Learning Curve
Leave A Message

Leave 'Em Laughing
Leave It To Chance
L'Ecole Du Coeur
Left Holding The Bag
Leftovers
Left With A Legacy
Legacy
Legal Eagle
Legalese
Legal Jargon
Legally Liable
Legal Tender
Legatee
Legendary
Legend Has It
Legend In My Time
Legend In Time
Legionaire
Leisure Time
Lenox
Leonardo
L'Esprit
Let Freedom Ring
Let Loose
Let's Boogie

Let's Dance
Let's Make A Deal
Let's Party
Let's Pretend
Let's Talk Turkey
Letterman
Letter Perfect
Letter To The Editor
Let The Good
    Times Roll
Let There Be Light
Levi
Levitator
Leviticus
Lexington
Lexus
Liar's Poker
Liberty
Liberty Valence
Lickety Split
Life Is A Cabaret
Life Is Peachy
Life Of The Party
Lifesaver
Lifestyle

Lifetime Contract
Lifetime Guarantee
Lighter Than Air
Lighthearted
Light In The Window
Lightning
Lightning Bolt
Lightning Rod
Lightning Strikes
Light Of Day
Light Show
Lights Out
Light The Torch
Light Touch
Like A Bandit
Like A Charm
Like A Rock
Like A Trojan
Like Magic
Likewise
Lilac Sky
Limelight
Limerick
Limited Edition
Limited Partnership

Lindbergh
Linebacker
Line Item Veto
Line Of Duty
Lionheart
Lion's Share
Liquid Asset
Listen Here
Listen Mister
Listen Up
List Price
Lit From Within
Lithographic Print
Living Legend
Living Will
Loaded Dice
Local Favorite
Local Legend
Locally Grown
Local Motion
Local Yocal
Lock, Stock And Barrel
Logically Speaking
Logo

Log On
London Calling
London Nights
London Times
Lone Ranger
Long Awaited
Long Distance Call
Long Distance Calling
Long Distance Operator
Long Johns
Long Overdue
Long Range Plan
Longshot
Long Time
Look Alive
Lookie Here
Looking Good
Looking Up
Look Of Knowledge
Looks Are Deceiving
Looks Could Kill
Look Twice
Loophole
Loose Change

Loose Lips
Loosey Goosey
Lord Of The Rings
Los Lobos
Lost Art
Lost For Words
Lost In Space
Lost My Shirt
Lots A Heart
Lots A Moxie
Lots Of Charisma
Lots Of Chutzpah
Lots Of Hype
Lots Of Publicity
Lots Of Savvy
Lots Of Soul
Lottery Ticket
Louvre
Lovelace
Love Letter
Love 'N Laughter
Love Notes
Love Of My Life
Love Potion
Lover Of Luxury

Love Song
Lowell
Low Risk
Loyalty
Luck Of The Draw
Luck Of The Irish
Lucky Charm
Lucky Day
Lucky Discovery
Lucky Draw
Lucky Duck
Lucky Hand
Lucky Number
Lucky Star
Lucky Strike
Ludwig
Lullaby
Lullaby Of Broadway
Luminescence
Lunar Eclipse
Luxurious
Luxury Item
Luxury Of Time
Luxury Tax
Lyric

Macarena
Macaroon
Mac Attack
Macchiato
MacDougal
MacIntosh
MacIntyre
Macon
Mad About You
Madcap Comics
Made For Me
Made From Scratch
Made In The Shade
Made The Grade
Made The Team
Made To Order
Madison Avenue
Mad Scientist
Maelstrom
Maestro
Mafioso

Magic Act
Magical Moment
Magic Carpet
Magic Carpet Ride
Magic Cure
Magic Dragon
Magic Maker
Magic Moment
Magic Phrase
Magic Potion #9
Magic Spell
Magic Spirit
Magic Spiritwater
Magic Touch
Magic Twist
Magic Wand
Magic Word
Magna Carta
Magna Cum Laude
Magnanimous
Magnanimous
    Gesture
Magnetic
Magnetic Attraction
Magnetic Charm

Magnetic Force
Magnetism
Magnolia Blossom
Mahogany
Mai Tai
Main Act
Main Attraction
Main Chance
Main Character
Main Course
Main Event
Main Feature
Mainframe
Main Squeeze
Main Stay
Main Street
Main Street
    Attraction
Maitre 'D
Majestic
Major Alliance
Major Ambition
Major Change
Major Enhancement
Majority Rules

Major Motion Picture
Major Replica
Major Sequel
Major Stockholder
Make A Dent
Make A Difference
Make Amends
Make A Move
Make An Effort
Make An Impression
Make A Statement
Make A Wish
Make Believe
Make Do
Make Me A Believer
Make Me A Deal
Make Me An Offer
Make Me Laugh
Make My Day
Makeover
Make Pretend
Make The Cut
Make The Deadline
Make The Grade
Make-Up Artist

Make Us Happy
Make Us Proud
Making Amends
Making An
    Impression
Making A Statement
Making Contacts
Making Headlines
Making History
Making Moolah
Making News
Making Plans
Making The Circuit
Making Waves
Malachi's Wisdom
Maltese Falcon
Manchester
Mandalay
Manhattan
Manhattan Style
Manhattan Transfer
Manifest Destiny
Manifesto
Man On The Moon
Mantra

Marching On
Marching Order
March Madness
March On
March Violets
Mardi Gras
Margin Call
Marimba
Mariposa
Marked Money
Market's Rising
Market Street
Market Value
Marking Time
Mark My Word
Mark Of Excellence
Marquis
Marquis De Sade
Marrakech Express
Mars Attack
Mars Bar
Marshmallow
Martial Art
Martini
Martini With A Twist

Mascot
Masquerade
Mass Exodus
Master Copy
Master Of
    Ceremonies
Master Of The Line
Mastermind
Masterpiece
Master Plan
Matchmaker
Match Play
Match Point
Material Witness
Math Blaster
Math Equation
Matinee Idol
Matter Of Fact
Matter Of Time
Matters Of Chance
Maverick
Max Factor
Maximum Clearance
Maximum Overdrive
Maximum Speed

Maximum Strength
Maximilian
Maxwell House
Mayflower
May Showers
Maze Craze
Mazerati
McDuffy
McGeorge
McPherson
Meadowbrook
Meadowlark
Means Of
    Comparison
Meant To Be
Measure Of Success
Mecca
Medford
Medicine Man
Medium Cool
Medium Hot
Medley
Meeting Street
Meet The Press
Mega Bytes

Megahertz
Mega Memory
Meister
Melodramatic
Memoir
Memory Lane
Memory Lapse
Memphis
Mendlesohn
Mental Edge
Mental Image
Mercedes
Mercedes Benz
Mercury Rising
Mercy, Mercy Me
Mere Mortal
Meridian
Merlin The Magician
Merlot
Merriment
Merry Go Round
Merrymaid
Mesmerized
Message In A Bottle
Message Machine

Message To Garcia
Messenger
Metamorphosis
Metaphor
Meteor
Meteorite
Meterologist
Method Of Operation
Methuselah
Meticulous Rhythm
Me Too
Metro Express
Metronome
Metropolis
Miami Vice
Miata
Micelob
Michigan Shuffle
Midas Touch
Middleground
Middleman
Middle Of The Road
Midlife Crisis
Midsummer Night's
    Dream

Midway
Mighty Ruler
Mignon
Mikado
Miles To Go
Milestone
Milkshake
Millennia
Millennium
Million Laughs
Milwaukee
Mimosa
Mind Games
Mind Over Matter
Mindset
Mineral Water
Minestrone
Miniskirt
Minnesota Snowflake
Minor Detail
Minstrel Act
Mint Condition
Mint Julep
Miracle
Miracle Maker

Miracle Play
Miracle Worker
Mirage Moonlight
Mirror Image
Mirror, Mirror
Mischief Maker
Misprint
Missing In Action
Missing Link
Missing Pieces
Mission
    Accomplished
Mission Control
Mission Impossible
Mission Statement
Miss You
Mistaken Identity
Mistletoe
Mists Of Avalon
Mitigating
    Circumstances
Mixed Agenda
Mixed Message
Mmm, Mmm Good
Mockingbird

Mockingbird Hill
Mock Turtle
Model Citizen
Model Prisoner
Model Student
Model T
Modern Eyes
Modern Marvel
Modern Times
Modesty
Moet
Mohair
Moi?
Molasses
Mollycoddle
Molotov
Momento
Moment Of Truth
Momentous Occasion
Moment's Notice
Mon Ami
Monday Madness
Monday Monday
Monday Morning Blues
Monet

Monet's Impression
Money Back
    Guarantee
Money Line
Moneymaker
Money Manager
Money Order
Money Pit
Money Talks
Money To Burn
Money Tree
Monitor
Monitor Improvement
Monkey Business
Monogram
Monopoly
Monroe's Doctrine
Monsignor
Montana
Monte Blanc
Monte Carlo
Monte Claire
Monte Sucre
Montezuma
Monthly Dividend

Month Of Sundays
Montreal
Monumental Decision
Moocher
Mood Elevator
Mood Music
Moonlight Becomes
    Me
Moonlighter
Moonlighting
Moonlight Madness
Moonlight Sonata
Moon Over Miami
Moon River
Moonraker
Moonspell
Moonspinner
Moon Struck
Moon Walk
Moral Of The Story
Moral Support
Moravian Night
More Magic
More Power To You
More Than Likely

Morgan Le Fay
Morgan Spice Rum
Morning Light
Morning News
Morning Rounds
Morning Show
Morning Taps
Morse Code
Most Advanced
Most Expensive Gift
Most Likely To
    Succeed
Most Modern
Most Precious
Most Wanted
Mother Hubbard
Mother Nature
Motion Detector
Motion Study
Motion To Compel
Motion To Dispel
Motown
Moulin Rouge
Mountain Spring
Movado

Move Over
Move Over Rover
Moving Star
Moving Violation
Movin' On Up
MT.V.
Much Ado
Mucha Moola
Mud Puppy
Mud Slinger
Mulberry
Mulberry Days
Mulberry Street
Mulligan Stew
Mumbo Jumbo
Mum's The Word
Murdock
Murmur
Murphy Brown
Murphy's Law
Music Major
Music Maker
Music To My Ears
Must Be Magic
Must See

Must See To
    Appreciate
Must See To Believe
Mutual Consent
My Accomplishment
My Analyst
My Baby
My Best
My Best Friend
My Blue Heaven
My Bodyguard
My Compadre
My Cup Of Tea
My Day Off
My Destiny
My Escort
My Ex
My Expensive
    Little Hobby
My Fantasy
My Forté
My Funny Valentine
My Inheritance
My Intuition
My Lucky Day

My Mantra
My Mentor
My Philosophy
My Pleasure
My Prerogative
My R.V.
My Sidekick
My Soul To Keep
Mysterious
Mysterious
    Motivation
Mysterious Ways
Mystery
Mystery By Design
Mystery Date
Mystery Guest
Mystify
Mystique
My Therapy
My Time
My Treasure
My Valentine
My Way
My Will

N

Nacho
Naive
Name Brand
Named Desire
Name Game
Name Of The Game
Namesake
Name That Tune
Nantucket Sound
Narcissa
Narcissus
Narrator
NASDAQ
Nashville
Nashville News
Nasturtium
National Appeal
National Debt
National News
National Pride
Native New Yorker

Native Of The Area
Native Sun
Native Texan
Natural Ingredient
Natural Instinct
Naturally
Natural Reaction
Natural Selection
Natural Way
Natural Wonder
Nature's Way
Nautilus
Navajo
Navigator
Nearly Missed
Nearly New
Neater By Far
Necessity
Need For Speed
Need I Say More?
Needless Worry
Need To Know
Negotiator
Nemesis
Neptune

Nerves Of Steel
Nestle's Quick
Network
Networker
Network News
Never A Dull Moment
Never A Miss
Never Ask Why
Never Been Better
Never Better
Never Dull
Never Ending Story
Never Ever
Never Finer
Never Idle
Never Look Back
Never Satisfied
Never Say Never
Never Say No
Never The Less
Never Too Late
New Age
New Beginning
New Doctrine
New Edition

New Endeavor
New Era
Newest Acquaintance
Newest Gamble
New Frontier
New Heights
New Horizon
New Image
New Lease On Life
Newmarket
New Moon
New Perspective
Newport
New Recruit
Newsbrief
Newsflash
Newsmaker
Newsprint
Newsworthy
New Technology
Newton's Law
New Wave
New York Minute
New York News
Next Best

Next Flight
Next Frontier
Next In Line
Next Of Kin
Nice Touch
Nick Of Time
Night Duty
Night Hawk
Nightingale
Night Ranger
Night Shift
Night Worker
Nimble
Nimbus
Nine One One
Nineth Hole
Nine To Five
Ninety Proof
Ninja
Nintendo
Nirvana
Nissan
Nittany Lion
Nitty Gritty
Noah

No Apologies
No Apologies Needed
Noble Prize
Noblesse Oblige
Nobility
Nobody's Business
Nobody's Child
Nobody's Fool
Nobody's Perfect
No Comment
No Complaints
No Contest
No Cover Charge
No Decision
No Deduction
No Deposit
No Return
No Detour
No Doubt
No Doubt About It
No Duplicate
No Effort
Noel
No Escape
No False Hope

No Fear
No Finance Charge
No Frills
No Guarantee
No Hoax
No Holds Barred
No Imagination
No Kidding
No Laughing Matter
No Limit
No Matter What
Nom De Plume
No Name
Nonillion
None Better
Nonesuch
None-The-Less
Non Fiction
Non-Negotiable
No Nonsense
No Offense
Nonpareil
Non-Profitable
Non-Refundable
Non-Returnable

Non-Sequitor
No Preservatives
No Preservatives
    Added
No Problem
No Questions Asked
No Refunds
No Remorse
No Reply
Norfolk
Normandy Beach
North By Northwest
Northern Crown
Northern Exposure
Northern Haze
Northern Lights
Northern Most Part
Northern Winds
No Service Charge
No Shame
No Shenanigans
Nostalgia
No Strings Attached
No Such Thing
No Sweat

Notebook
Noted Scholar
Noteworthy
Noteworthy Opponent
Not For Hire
Not Guilty
Nothin' But The Truth
Nothin' But The Best
Nothing Fancy
Nothing To Chance
Nothing To Lose
Notice Of Intent
Not My Fault
Not On Your Life
Notoriety
Notorious
Not To Worry
No Turning Back
Nouveau Riche
Nova
Novel Idea
November Rain
Now Appearing
No Way
No Way Out

No Wonder
Now Or Never
Nucleus
Numbers Runner
Numero Uno
Nutmeg
N.Y.P.D.
N.Y. Yankee

Oasis
Oath Of Allegiance
Obelisk
Obey The Law
Object At hand
Objet D'Art
Obliging
Oblique
Oblivious
Obscure Meaning
Obsessed
Obsession
Obvious

Obvious Choice
Obvious Ending
Obvious Intentions
Occupant
Occupied
Ocean Breeze
Oddfellow
Odds Are
Odds On Favorite
Odyssey
Of Course
Off Broadway
Off Camera
Officer In Charge
Off Limits
Off The Clock
Off The Cuff
Off The Hook
Off The Rack
Off The Record
Off The Top
Of Paramount
   Importance
Of Public Matter
Oh Contraire

Oh My Gosh
Oh Promise Me
Oh So Cool
Oh So Fine
Oh Thank Heaven
OK By Me
Okeydoke
Old Dominion
Old Faithful
Old Fashioned
Old Money
Olympian
Omaha
Omega
Omega Force
Omega Three
Omnibus
Ominous
Ominous Thunder
Omniscient
On A Mission
On A Pedestal
On Approval
On A Promise
On A Roll

On A Scholarship
On A Shoestring
On Assignment
Onassis
On A Whim
On Borrowed Time
On Broadway
On Call
On Camera
On Capitol Hill
Once In A While
Once Removed
Once Upon A Time
On Command
On Commission
On Credit
On Cue
On Deck
On Demand
On Display
One And Only
One-Derful
One Fell Swoop
One Fine Day
One For All

One For The Money
One For The Road
One Hundred Proof
One In A Million
One Moment In Time
One More Time
One Night In Bangkok
One Night Stand
One No Trump
One Of A Kind
One Of The Best
One Of The Crowd
One Of These Days
One Shining Moment
One Step Above
One Step Ahead
One Step Closer
One Step Up
One Thin Dime
One Tin Soldier
One Track Mind
One Way Ticket
On Guard
On Hand
Online

On Location
Only Chance
Only Fitting
Only Game In Town
Only Speculation
Only The Best
Only The Lonely
On My Honor
On My Mind
On My Own
On Occasion
Onomatopoeia
On Request
On Restriction
On Salary
On Schedule
On Second Thought
On Speculation
On Stage
On Strike
On Tap
On Target
On The Bandwagon
On The Bayou
On The Bench

On The Bright Side
On The Brink
On The Button
On The Cusp
On The Double
On The Edge
On The Go
On The Horizon
On The Internet
On The Job
On The Lam
On The Level
On The Line
On The Loose
On The Money
On The Move
On The Offense
On The Other Hand
On The Payroll
On The Prowl
On The Q.T.
On The Rebound
On The Right Track
On The Road Again
On The Rocks

On The Run
On The Sly
On The Take
On The Town
On The Up And Up
On The Verge
On The Way
On Thin Ice
On Time
On Top
On Tour
On Track
On Trial
On Your Mark
On Your Merry Way
On Your Side
On Your Toes
Open For Business
Open Handed
Open Hearted
Opening Act
Opening Bid
Opening Ceremony
Opening Line
Opening Night

Left: Centella. Photo contributed by Paulette Mouchet, Crown Valley Press of Acton, CA.
Above right: Autumn. Photo contributed by Suzanne Drnec of Chino, CA
Lower right: Sonya's Cherokee Maiden. Photo contributed by Sonya Austin, American Part-Blooded Horse Registry of Portland, OR.

Opening Statement
Open Invitation
Open Options
Open Season
Open Secret
Open To Suggestion
Opera Buff
Opera Fan
Opinionated
Opinionated One
Opium
Opulent
Opportunistic
Opportunity Waits
Opportunity Knocks
Opposite Attraction
Opposites Attract
Optical Illusion
Optimum
    Performance
Optimum Pride
Opulent Attitude
Oracle
Orchestrator
Order In Advance

Order In The Court
Orderly Fashion
Ordinary World
Oregano
Or Else
Orient Express
Original Flavor
Orion
Ornamental
Orwellian
Oscar Winner
Other Side Of The
    Tracks
O'Toole
Ouija
Outcast
Outer Bank
Outer Limits
Outfielder
Outfoxed
Outlook
Out Of Character
Out Of L.A.
Out Of Nowhere
Out Of Print

Out Of Sight
Out Of The Blue
Out Of The North
Out Of The Ordinary
Out Of The Park
Out Of The Past
Out Of The Question
Out Of This World
Outrageous Reasoning
Outside Influence
Outside Sails
Outspoken
Outstanding
Outta Here
Outta The Blue
Outta This World
Out To Lunch
Outward Bound
Overabundance
Overachiever
Overdrive
Over Ice
Overkill
Overnight Guest
Overnight Sensation

Overnight Success
Overseas
Over The Candlestick
Over The Edge
Over The Fence
Over The Hill
Over The Horizon
Over The Rainbow
Over The Legal Limit
Over The Limit
Overtime
Own Agenda
Owner's Equity
Own Recognizance
Oy Vey
Oxford Blue
Oxford Grad
Ozark Exile
Ozone Layer

P

Pace Yourself
Pacific Pride
Pacific Sun
Pacific Time
Pac Man
Packaged Goods
Packard
Paddington Station
Paddy Wagon
Pagemaster
Page One
Page Turner
Pagoda
Paid In Full
Pajama Party
Palimony
Palladium
Pampered
Panache
Panama
Panasonic

Panavision
Panorama
Pantomime
Paparazzi
Papaya
Paperback Writer
Paper Boy
Paper Moon
Paper Pusher
Paper Tiger
Paper Trail
Papillon
Paprika
Parade Master
Paradigm
Paradise
Paradox
Paragon
Paragon Of Virtue
Parallel View
Paramount
Paramour
Par Avion
Parcheesi
Parchment

Pardon Me
Pardon My French
Pardonnes Moi
Par Excellence
Par For The Course
Par Four
Paris Calls
Park Avenue
Park Place
Parliamentary
    Procedure
Parody
Parsley
Part Of The Plan
Partner In Crime
Party Lights
Party Line
Party Time
Passer By
Passing
    Acquaintance
Passionate Kiss
Passionate Pursuit
Passion For Detail
Passkey

Passport
Passport To Paris
Pass The Buck
Pass The Word
Password
Past Issues
Past Participle
Patented
Patent Pending
Pathfinder
Pathological Liar
Patron Of The Arts
Patternmaker
Pause For Affect
Pawn Shop Special
Payback
Paycheck
Pay Day
Pay Dearly
Pay Dirt
Pay In Cash
Paying Tribute
Payment Plan
Pay The Price
P.C.

P.D.Q.
Peace Child
Peace Of Mind
Peace Treaty
Peaches
Peachy Keen
Peanuts
Pedal Pusher
Pedal To The Metal
Peer Group
Peer Pressure
Peerless
Pegasus
Pencil Me In
Pending Approval
Pending Action
Pendleton
Pennant Fever
Penny Pincher
Pennywise
Pentagon
Pentagon Papers
Penthouse Suite
People Are Talking
People's Choice

Peppercorn
Pepperoni
Pep Talk
Perchance
Per Diem
Perennial
Perfect Alibi
Perfect Attendance
Perfect Harmony
Perfectly Clear
Perfectly Content
Perfectly Right
Perfect Match
Perfect Partner
Perfect Plan
Perfect Posture
Perfect Remedy
Perfect Replica
Perfect Saint
Perfect Sense
Perfect Setting
Perfect Solution
Perfect Timing
Perfect Touch
Perfect Union

Performance Plus
Performing Act
Peridot
Periwinkle
Perjury
Permanent Attraction
Permanent Feature
Permanent Fun
Permission Granted
Permission Slip
Pernod
Perpetual Light
Perpetual Motion
Perrier
Per Se
Perseus
Perseverance
Persian Flaw
Persimmons
Persistent
Personal Best
Personal Charm
Personal Coach
Personal Favorite
Personal Investment

Personality Plus
Personal Obsession
Personal Preference
Personal Space
Personal Touch
Personal Trainer
Personified Soul
Persuasion
Persuasive
Pertinent Info
Pet Peeve
Petite Ange
Petit Four
Petty Cash
Peugeot
Phantom
Phantom Of The
   Opera
Phenomenal One
Phenomenon
Philabuster
Philadelphia Eagle
Philadelphia Freedom
Philadelphia Lawyer
Philosopher

Phoenix
Phoenix Sun
Phone Home
Phoney Bologna
Photo Finish
Photographic Memory
Photo Opportunity
Photogenic
Photostat
Physical Attraction
Picasso
Piccadilly
Piccadilly Circus
Picked At Random
Pickled Peppers
Pickwick Papers
Picture Perfect
Picture This
Picturesque
Piece De Resistance
Piece Of Mind
Pie In The Sky
Pier One
"Pie" Squared
Pilfering Pennies

Pilgrim's Pride
Pilot Program
P.I.N.
Pinafore
Pinball Wizard
Ping Pong
Pink Champagne
Pinkerton
Pink Panther
Pink Surprise
Pinnacle
Pinot Grigio
Pipe Down
Pipe Dream
Pirouette
Pisces
Pistashio
Pivotal Point
Pizazz
P. J. McQuay
Plains Of Savannah
Plain Speaking
Plain Talk
Plain Truth
Plan "A"

Plan Ahead
Plan "B"
Planet Hollywood
Planet "X"
Plan Of Action
Plantiff's Plea
Playback
Playboy Bunny
Play Fair
Play For Keeps
Playful
Playing It Cool
Playing It Straight
Playing For Keeps
Playing Second Fiddle
Play It Again Sam
Play It By Ear
Play Me Right
Plea Bargain
Plead The Fifth
Pleasant Memory
Pleasant Surprise
Please Be Seated
Pledge Of Allegiance
Plentiful

Plum Pudding
Plum Tuckered
Pocket Change
Pocketful Of Miracles
Pocketful Of Posies
Poetic Justice
Poetic License
Poet Lauriat
Poetry In Motion
Point Counterpoint
Point In Question
Point Of Honor
Point Of No Return
Point Of Reference
Point Of View
Point Spread
Points For Originality
Polaris
Policy Maker
Polished Brass
Politically Correct
Poco
Polygram
Pontiac
Pop Art

63

Poppagallo
Popular Demand
Popularity Contest
Por Favor
Porsche
Portfolio
Port Of Freedom
Poseidon
Positive Influence
Positively Priceless
Positive Step
Post Haste
Postmaster
Potpourri
Pouilly-Fuisse
Powder
Power Broker
Powerhouse
Power Of Attorney
Power Of Suggestion
Power Play
Power Source
Powers That Be
Power Surge
Practical Joker

Practically Perfect
Praiseworthy
Pray Tell
Precious Cargo
Precious Few
Precious Moment
Precious Relic
Precision Tool
Predicting Storms
Preferential
    Treatment
Preferred Property
Preferred Remedy
Preferred Risk
Preferred Stock
Prelude
Premier Attraction
Premiere
Premier Occasion
Premonition
Prenuptial Agreement
Preoccupied
Preposterous
Prescott
Prescribed Remedy

Prescription For
    Stress
Present Tense
Presidental Pardon
President Elect
Press Pass
Press Proof
Press Release
Press Reporter
Prestige
Prestigious
Presto Chango
Presumptious
Pretzel
Presumed Innocent
Pretender
Pretense
Pretty Daring
Pretty Please
Preview
Priceless
Priceless Commodity
Priceless Heirloom
Priceless Moment
Priceless Treasure

Pricey
Primal Influence
Prime Candidate
Prime Minister
Prime Rate
Prime Source
Prime Suspect
Prime Time
Primrose Lane
Primrose Path
Pringles
Prior Record
Prism Reflections
Prisoner Of Rhythm
Private Affair
Private Agreement
Private Asset
Private Carrier
Private Collection
Private Eye
Private Label
Private Passion
Private Property
Private Reserve
Private Sale

Private Screening
Private Stash
Private Stock
Private Treaty
Private View
Privilege
Privileged Character
Prized Possession
Prize Package
Prizzi's Honor
Proactive
Pro Bono
Proclamation
Prodigal Son
Professional
   Courtesy
Professionally
   Speaking
Profile In Courage
Pro Forma
Progress Report
Promised Land
Promise Keeper
Promise Land
Promise Me

Promises Promises
Promising Future
Promissory Note
Proof Of Purchase
Proof Positive
Proofreader
Proper English
Prophecy
Propitious
Prosperity
Prosperous
Protégé
Protocol
Proof Positive
Proof Ready
Propaganda
Prophesy
Prototype
Proud As Punch
Proud Flight
Proud Petunia
Proverb
Providence
Proving Ground
P.S.

P.S. I Love You
Psychedelic
Psychic
Public Affair
Public Display
Public Enemy
   Number One
Public Image
Publicity Hound
Publicity Stunt
Public Knowledge
Public Notice
Public Occasion
Public Opinion
Pulitzer Prize
Pulp Fiction
Pulse Rate
Pumpernickel
Punchline
Pure Magic
Pursuit
Pursuit Of Happiness
Pursuit Of Honor
Pushing The
   Envelope

Push The Limit
Put The Moves On
Putting On The Ritz
Pygmalion

Quadrille
Quaint Gesture
Quaker's Meeting
Qualified
Quality Control
Quality Diamond
Quality Time
Quandary
Quantum Leap
Quantum Reality
Quantum Theory
Quarterback Sneak
Quarter Dollar
Quasar
Queen's Guard
Que Sera
Quest For Knowledge

CC Anja Chiffon is bred by Cedar Coulee Pintabians. The names of all foals raised on this ranch begin with the letters "CC" for Cedar Coulee. Photo contributed by Pintabian Horse Registry of Karlstad, MN.

Quick Thinking
Quid Pro Quo
Quiescence
Quiet Please
Quiet Riot
Quiet Solitude
Quiet Touch
Quietism
Quietude
Quikdraw McGraw
Quite A Catch
Quite The Contrary
Quitting Time
Quixote
Quizmaster
Quiz Show Host
Quizzical
Quotation Mark
Quote Of The Day

Quest For The Best
Quibble
Quick Change Artist
Quick Delivery
Quick Pik
Quicksand
Quick Solution
Quick Study

R

Racketeer
Radar
Radar Enforced
Radar Ranger
Radiant
Radical Change
Radical Dude
Radcliffe
Radio Flyer
Raffia
Raffles
Ragin' Cajun
Raging Passion
Raging Romance
Rags To Riches
Ragtime
Rain Check
Rain Dancer
Rain Shower
Rainbow
Rainbow's End

Rainfall
Rainforest
Rainmaker
Rainman
Rainy Day
Rainy Tuesday
Raise The Roof
Raise The Stakes
Raleigh
Rambler
Ramblin' On
Rameses
Ramsey
Random Access
Random Chance
Random Choice
Range Rover
Ransom
Rapid Transit
Rare Adventure
Rare Air
Rare Collectible
Rare Mettle
Rare Opportunity
Rarer Still

Rare Secret
Rasmussen
Rasputin
Rated PG
Rated R
Rated X
Rational Thoughts
Rave Review
Raw Deal
Raw Material
Raw Power
Razor Sharp
Razzle Dazzle
Razzmatazz
R.B.I.
Reach Out
Read It And Weep
Read Me A Story
Read My Lips
Ready For Action
Ready For Anything
Ready For Take-Off
Ready Or Not
Ready, Set, Go
Real Country

Real Cute
Real Deal
Realistic
Realistic Goal
Reality Check
Real Life
Really Secret
Real McCoy
Realms Of Glory
Real Quick
Real Secret
Rear Admiral
Reasonable Doubt
Reason To Believe
Reason To Celebrate
Rebate
Rebel
Rebel Ghost
Rebel Leader
Rebellious
Rebel Rouser
Rebound
Recent Addition
Recent Past
Recommended List

Recorded Message
Record High
Recreational Vehicle
Redeeming Value
Redemption
Rediscovery
Reel Steel
Reference Point
Refinance
Reflections
Reflective
Reggae Rhythm
Regrets Only
Reigning Authority
Reigning Royalty
Reigning Ruler
Reinforcements
Reiterate That
Rejuvenation
Relativity
Relentless
Rely On The Tiger
Remarkable
R.E.M. Dreams
Remember Me

Remember When
Remington
Reminiscent
Renaissance
Renaissance Artist
Rendezvous
Rendition
Renegade
Renown
Repeat After Me
Repeat Performance
Replica
Reporting On Duty
Reprisal
Reserved
Reserved Rights
Reserved Seat
Residual
Resisted Arrest
Resolution
Resourceful
Resource Specialist
R.E.S.P.E.C.T.
Responder
Rest Assured

67

Restless
Restraining Order
Restricted
Resultz R In
Resurrection
Retroactive
Return Engagement
Revealed Secret
Revealing Ways
Reveille
Revelation
Revered
Reverse The Charges
Revivalist
Revolution
Revolutionary
Revolutionist
Revolving Credit
Rhapsody
Rhapsody In Blue
Rhetoric
Rhinestone Cowboy
Rhodes Scholar
Rhododendron
Rhyme In Time

Rhyme Nor Reason
Rhyming Lyrcs
Ribbon Fair
Richmond
Ricochet
Riddled With Guilt
Riddle Me This
Ride The Surf
Ride The Tide
Riding My
    Inheritance Away
Riding Shotgun
Riff Raff
Rigamarole
Right As Rain
Right Chemistry
Right In Style
Rightly So
Right On
Right On Target
Right On Time
Right To Rule
Ring A Bell
Ringer
Ringleader

Ringmaster
Ring My Bell
Ripple Effect
Riptide
Rise Above It
Rising Costs
Rising Fever
Rising Interests
Rising Market
Rising Rainbow
Rising Rates
Rising Star
Rising Sun
Rising Waters
Risky Business
Rites Of Passage
Riverboat Gambler
Riviera
Riverwalk
Riverdancer
Riviera
Road Runner
Roadster
Road To Memphis
Road To Riches

Road To Success
Road To The Garden
Road Warrior
Robotix
Rochambeau
Rocheleau
Rochester
Rocket Scientist
Rockford Files
Rocky Road
Rockwell
Rodeo
Role Model
Role Play
Role Reversal
Roll Call
Rolling Stone
Roll Of The Dice
Roll Out The Red
    Carpet
Rolls Royce
Rolodex
Roman Days
Romancer
Romancing The Stone

Roman Holiday
Roman Numeral
Roman Warrior
Rom Dos
Rome On Fire
Rootin' Tootin'
  Cowboy
Rorschach
Rorschach Test
R.O.T.C.
Rothchild
Rouge Et Noir
Rough Copy
Rough Cut
Rough Magic
Roulette
Round About
Round And Round
Roundelay's Beauty
Round Robin
Round Table
Round The Bend
Round Trip Ticket
Roving Reporter
Royal Affair

Royal Brigade
Royal Cadence
Royal Charter
Royal Class
Royal Crest
Royal Crown
Royal Crusader
Royal Dalton
Royal Flush
Royal Image
Royal Knight
Royal Lad
Royal Occasions
Royal Order
Royal Rites
Royal Secret
Royal T.
Rule Breaker
Rule Of Thumb
Rules Of The Game
Rumor
Rumor Has It
Rumor Mill
Rum Raisin
Rumrunner

Running For Office
Running Waters
Run Of Luck
Run The Gamut
Russian Roulette
Rustabout
Rutledge
Rutherford

S

Sachet
Sacramento
Sacred Object
Sacrificial Lamb
Safari
Sage Advice
Said and Done
Sailing Along
Sailmaker
Sailor Moon
Sailor's Delight
Sail With The Stars
Saintly

Saks Fifth Avenue
Salt Of The Earth
Salt Water Taffy
Salute
Sambuca
Same Old, Same Old
Same Old Tune
Same Page
Same Wavelength
Sample
Samurai
Samurai Warrior
San Antonio Spur
Sanctuary
San Francisco Treat
San Jose Shark
Sapphire's Song
Saratoga
Sasha
Sasparilla
Sassoon
Satchmo
Satellite Signal
Satin Finish
Satin Sheets

69

Saturday Matinee
Saturday Morning
  Cartoon
Saturday Night Fever
Saturday Night
  Special
Saucy Aussie
Sauvignon
Savannah's Moon
Savior Faire
Savoy
Savvy
Sayonora
Say Cheese
Say My Prayers
Say No More
Say's Who
Say The Magic Word
Say Your Prayers
Scandalous
Scandal Sheet
Scarborough Fair
Scenario
Scene II
Scene Stealer

Scenic Wonder
Scheduled For
  Take-Off
Scheme Of Things
Schmooz'n
Scholarly Ways
Schubert
Schumacher
Schweppes Tonic
Science Fair
Science Fiction
Scientific American
Scientific
  Breakthrough
Scintilla
Scintillated Affair
Scintillation
Scorcher Day
Scoreboard
Scotch Guard
Scotland Yard
Scottish Mist
Scottsdale
Scoundrel
Scout's Honor

Scrabble
Screaming Mimi
Screen Play
Screen Test
Screenwriter
Scrimmage
Scrumptious
Scrunchy
Sea Breeze
Sealed Bid
Seal Of Approval
Search For Tomorrow
Season Premiere
Season's Greetings
Season's Pass
Season To Taste
Seattle
Sebastian
Second Assault
Second Balcony
Second Chair
Second Chance
Second Cousin
Second Edition
Second Effort

Second Generation
Second Glance
Second Guess
Second In Command
Second Look
Second Mortgage
Second Nature
Second Opinion
Second Sight
Second Step
Second Story
Second Tenor
Second Term
Second That Emotion
Second The Motion
Second Thoughts
Second Time Around
Second To None
Secret Admirer
Secret Agent
Secret Agent Man
Secret Ballot
Secret Code
Secret Formula
Secret Gift

Secret Handshake
Secret Ingredient
Secret Message
Secret Of Success
Secret Passage
Secret Passion
Secret Password
Secret Past
Secret Project
Secret Revealed
Secret Rendezvous
Secret Service Agent
Secret Smile
Secret Society
Secret Surrealist
Secret Trust
Secret Weapon
Security Deposit
Security Funds
Security Risk
Seeks Applause
Seeing Is Believing
See The Light
Segue
Se Habla Espanol

Seinfeld
Seize The Day
Seldom Heard
Seldom Seen
Select Few
Self Image
Self-Insured
Self Portrait
Self Propelled
Seltzer
Semester Break
Seminar Topic
Semi Pro
Semi-Sweet
Send My Regards
Seniority
Sensational
Sense Of Direction
Sense Of Honor
Sense Of Humor
Sense Of Irony
Sensitivity Trainer
Sentimental Favorite
Sentimental Journey
Sepia Finish

Sequel
Sequestered Jury
Serenade
Serendipity
Serenity
Serious Moment
Serious Thinker
Serve Notice
Service Manager
Set Free
Set In Stone
Set Point
Set Sail
Set The Beat
Set The Limit
Set The Pace
Set The Precedent
Set The Stage
Set The Standard
Set The Style
Set The Tempo
Setting Sail
Seven Come Eleven
Seventh Heaven
Seville

Shadywood
Shake It Up
Shalimar
Shall We Dance
Shameless
Shame On You
Shamrock
Shamrock Sea
Shandy
Shangri-La
Shannondoah
Share The Limelight
Share The Wealth
Sharper Image
Shawnee
Sheboygan
Sheer Magic
Sheer Sense
Sheherazad
Shenanigans
Sherwood
Shifting Gears
Shifting Sands
Shifting Winds
Shimmer

Shimmering
Shine On Me
Shining Hour
Shining Moment
Shining Path
Shiny Side Up
Ship Ahoy
Shipshape
Shisheido
Shock Value
Shock Wave
Shoe In
Shogun
Shooting Star
Shoot The Moon
Shoot To Kill
Shop Talk
Shortcake
Short Circuit
Shot In The Dark
Show Biz
Showcase
Showdown
Showing Talent
Show Me The Money

Show Me The Way
Show No Fear
Show No Mercy
Show Off
Show Of Faith
Showtime
Shut Out
Shutter Speed
Shuttle Service
Shyster
Side Effects
Sideshow
Siegfried
Siesta Time
Signal Light
Signal Point
Signature
Signed, Sealed
    & Delivered
Signed Truce
Significant Other
Sign Of The Times
Sign Of The Zodiac
Sight For Sore Eyes
Sightly

Sightseer
Sight Unseen
Sign Language
Silence Please
Silent Auction
Silent Partner
Silent Juror
Silent Majority
Silent Partner
Silent Sky
Silent Storm
Silent Watch
Silhouette
Silk Stockings
Silk Tye
Silkwood
S'il Vous Plaît
Simpatico
Simple Excitement
Simple Faith
Simple Fool
Simple Melody
Simplicity
Simply Darling
Simply Irresistable

Simply Marvelous
Simply Speaking
Simply Splendid
Since One Day
Sincerely
Sincerely Yours
Sincerity
Sin City
Sinclair
Sing-A-Long
Singleminded
Sing Me A Song
Sing The Blues
Sing Your Praises
Sittin' Pretty
Sixth Sense
Sketch Artist
Sky Captain
Skye Walker
Sky High
Sky High Airway
Skylark
Skyline
Skylink
Skynet

Skyrocket
Skyscape
Slap Me Five
Slapshot
Slap Stick
Slavedriver
Sleeper
Sleepless In Seattle
Sleepy Head
Sleighride
Sleight Of Hand
Sleuth
Slider
Slight Twist
Slim Chance
Slow Dance
Slow Motion
Slowly But Surely
Sly Lock Fox
Sly One
Smart Angle
Smart Appearance
Smart Cookie
Smart Dresser
Smell The Roses

Smog Free
Smooth As Silk
Smoothie
Smooth Illusions
Smooth Move
Smooth Operator
Smooth Sailing
S'More
Snap Decision
Snapdragon
Snappy Dresser
Snappy Tune
Snapshot
Snap Shot
Snap To It
Sneak A Peek
Sneak Preview
Sneaky
Snooze You Loose
Soapbox
Soap Opera Hero
Soaring Eagle
So Be It
Sob Story
Social Butterfly

Social Climber
Social Graces
Social Integrity
Social Security
Social Studies
So Fine
So Fun
So Gauche
So Jaded
Solar Eclipse
Solar Flare
Solar Power

*Captain and Wendy Dowling.
Photo contributed by Catherine
Lewis of Petaluma, CA.*

*VooDoo. The Belgian Warmblood Breeding Association names
their foals according to the year of birth. All foals of the same
birth year are named with the same first letter. "V" (VooDoo) is
for foals born in 1998. Photo contributed by the Belgian
Warmblood Breeders Association of Chapin, SC.*

Solar Rings
Solar Wind
Sold Out
Soldier Blue
Soldier Of Fortune
Sole Survivor
Solemn Promise
Solidarity
Solid Citizen
Solid Solution
Solid State
Soliloquy
Solitaire
Solitude
Solo
Solo Flight
So Lucky
Somebody
Somebody New
Someday
Someday Soon
Somersby
Somerset
Something Brewing
Something Else

Something Good
Something Nice
Something Of Value
Something Special
Something's Up
Something To Talk
    About
Song Of Sixpence
Sonic Boom
Sooner Or Later
Soothsayer
So Rare
Sorcerer's Apprentice
Sorceress
Sorrel Ridge
So Sexy
So Slim
Sotheby
Soul Mate
Soul Searcher
Soul Survivor
Soul Train
Sound Advice
Sound Doctrine
Sound Of Silence

Sound Reasoning
Soundwaves
Soup To Nuts
Sourball
Source Of Energy
Southbound Express
Southern Accent
Southern Charm
Southern Comfort
Southern Cross
Southern Crown
Southern Drawl
Southern Exposure
Southern Magnolia
Southern Pines
South Kent
South Of Market
South Street
So Vain
Souvenir
Souvenir Copy
Souvenir Issue
Sovereign
Sovereign Chance
Sovereign Ruler

So What!
Space Cadet
Space Invader
Space Jam
Space Odyssey
Space Saver
Space Traveler
Spandex
Spare Change
Spare No Expense
Spare Nothing
Spare The Rod
Spark In The Dark
Sparkling Choice
Sparkling Cider
Sparkling Delight
Sparkling Gem
Spark Plug
Sparks Fly
Spartan
Speakeasy
Speaker Of The
    House
Speak No Evil
Special Assignment

Special Attention
Special Attraction
Special Bid
Special Case
Special Commission
Special Delivery
Special Dispatch
Special Edition
Special Effect
Special Effects
Special Envoy
Special Favors
Special Feeling
Special Guest
Special Invite
Special Liaison
Special Love
Special Model
Special News
Special Occasion
Special Order
Special Prosecutor
Special Recording
Special Request
Special T.

Special Touch
Specialty Of The House
Special Ways
Spectator
Speculation
Speculator
Spectacle
Speechless
Speech Maker
Speed Dial
Speed Of Light
Spellbinder
Spellbound
Spellspinner
Spencer
Spending Spree
Spendthrift
Sphere Of Influence
Spiced Just Right
Spice Of Life
Spiffy Dresser
Spill The Beans
Spindletop
Spin Doctor

Spinnaker
Spin Off
Spirit Guide
Spirit Of Adventure
Spirit Of Shiloh
Spirit Of St. Louis
Spirit World
Spitting Image
Splash
Splashdown
Splash Of Brilliance
Splash Of Lime
Splendiferous
Splendor In The Grass
Split Decision
Splitting Hairs
Spoiled Silly
Spontaneous
Spontaneous Combustion
Sport Authority
Sporting Chance
Sporting Spirit
Sport's Fan

Sport's Page
Sport's Report
Spreadsheet
Spread The News
Spring Bash
Spring Break
Spring Fever
Springfield
Spring Fling
Spring Into Action
Spring Rain
Spring Showers
Spring Song
Springtime In Paris
Sprig Of Mint
Spruced Goose
Spunkmeyer
Spunky
Spur Of The Moment
Spy Mission
Squadron Leader
Square Wheels
Squeaky Clean
Squire
S.R.O.

*Johnathon Lobell. Any Standardbred racehorse with a name containing
"Lobell" means the horse was bred at Lana Lobell Farms.
Photo contributed by Dawn Lyons of Montgomery, NY.*

Stable Economy
Stack The Deck
Stage Director
Stagehand
Stage Struck
Stage Whisper
Stained Glass
Stairway To Heaven
Stake Your Claim
Stamp Of Approval
Standard Deviation
Standard Issue
Stand By Me
Stand Firm
Standing Chance
Standing Firm
Standing Ovation
Standing Room Only
Standoffish
Stand Out
Stand Up And Cheer
Stand Up Comic
Stand Up Guy
Stansbury
Stanza

Starburst
Starfish
Stargazer
Starry Eyed
Starry Night
Starship Trooper
Star Struck
Start From Scratch
Starting Over
Star Trek
Stated Fact
Statement Of Fact
Statement Of Purpose
Staten Island
State Occasion
State Of Affairs
State Of Mind
State Of The Art
State Of The Union
State Secret
State's Evidence
State Trooper
Statuesque
Status Quo
Status Seeker

Status Symbol
Stay Tuned
Steadfast
Stealing Home
Steal The Show
Steamed Up
Steam Roller
Steelworker
Steinway
Stellar Performance
Step Aside
Step By Step
Step Lively
Stepping Out
Stepping Stone
Step Softly
Stereotype
Stetson
Stick With Me
Sticker Shock
Stiletto
Stiletto Stealth
Still The One
Still Waters
Stitch 'N Time

Stockbrocker
Stock Dividend
Stockholder
Stock In Trade
Stock Market
Stock Market Blues
Stockmarket Rising
Stock Option
Stock Phrase
Stolen Goods
Stolen Property
Stonehenge
Stone's Throw
Stool Pigeon
Stop The Clock
Stop The Music
Stop The Press
Stormy Monday
Story Book Ending
Storyville
Straight Arrow
Straight A's
Straight As An Arrow
Straight Laced
Straight Talk

Straight Up
Stranger In The Night
Stratavarius
Strategic Move
Strategic Planning
Strategy
Streak Of Luck
Streamlined
Stream Of Things
Stream Of
  Consciousness
Streetcar Named
  Desire
Street Dreams
Street Fighter
Street Legal
Street Level
Street Sign
Street Slang
Street Smart
Street Talk
Street Value
Street Wise
Stress Manager
Strictly Platonic

Strictly Speaking
Strike A Pose
Strike At Dawn
Strike Force
Strike Up The Band
Striking
Striking Image
Striking Resemblance
Stroke Of Genius
Stroke Of Luck
Strolling By
Struttin' My Stuff
Stuck On You
Studebaker
Study Hall
Stuff And Such
Stunning
Stunt Man
Subject To Approval
Subject To Change
Subliminal
  Advertising
Subliminal Message
Suburban Rhythm
Sub Zero

Success
Success In The Air
Success Story
Such Devotion
Sudden Appearance
Sudden Impact
Sudden Inspiration
Suddenly
Sudden Onset
Sugarfoot
Sugar Pie
Sugar Plum
Suit Yourself
Sukiyaki
Sullivan
Sultan
Sultan Of Swing
Summer Breeze
Summer Fancy
Summer Games
Summer Job
Summer Magic
Summer Night's
  Dream
Summer Place

Summer Rerun
Summer Rain
Summer Reign
Summer School
Summer Showers
Summer Squall
Summer Theme
Summer Tryst
Summer Wind
Sunday Best
Sunday Bonnet
Sunday Drive
Sunday Driver
Sunday Edition
Sunday In The
  Country
Sunday Meeting
Sunday Paper
Sunday's Best
Sunday's Surprise
Sunshine Forecast
Super Deluxe
Super Deluxe Model
Super Ego
Superficial

Super Hero
Superlative
Super Natural
Super Sleuth
Supersonic
Super Tramp
Supremacy
Sure Delight
Sure Enough
Sure Magic
Sure Shot
Sure Thing
Surf City
Surf's Up
Surf The Net
Surf The Waves
Surprise
Surprise Element
Surprise Ending
Surprise Package
Surprise Verdict
Surrealist
Surrender The
    Moment
Survey Results

Suspended In Space
Suspended In Time
Suspicious
Suspicious Person
Swan Song
S.W.A.K.
Sweepstakes Winner
Sweep The Nation
Sweet Ambrosia
Sweet Amnesia
Sweet Appeal
Sweet As Can Be
Sweet As Pie
Sweet Briar
Sweet Bitters
Sweet Deal
Sweet Desire
Sweet Dreams
Sweet Event
Sweetheart Deal
Sweet Mystery
    Of Life
Sweet Rain
Sweet Revenge
Sweet Spot

Sweet Sensation
Sweet Success
Sweet Talk
Sweet Temptation
Sweet Thing
Sweet Victory
Swept Away
Swing-A-Long
Swing Set
Swing Shift
Swiss Account
Swiss Air
Swiss Movement
Swiss Watch
Switching Gears
Swizzle
Symbolic
Symbolic Gesture
Symbolic Handshake
Symbolism
Symmetry
Sympatico
Symphony
Symposium
Syncopated Rhythm

Syndrome
Syndicated
Syndicated For
    Millions
Syndication
Synergy
Syntax Is Correct

*Woody and Lauren Santarella.
Photo contributed by Lauren
Santarella of Ridgefield, NJ.*

T

Table For Two
Table Manners
Table Talk
Tabloid Hero
Taboo
Taboo Topic
Tackles
Tacoma
Tactical Advantage
Tailgaiter
Tailspin
Tailwind
Tainted Evidence
Take A Bow
Take A Break
Take A Chance
Take A Look
Take Another Look
Take A Shot
Take A Stand
Take Care

Take Command
Take Heart
Take Heat
Take Heed
Take Home
Take It For Granted
Take It Or Leave It
Taken For A Ride
Take Notes
Takeover Bid
Takeover Target
Take The Field
Take The Heat
Take The Rapids
Take The Stand
Takes The Cake
Take Two
Takes Two To Tango
Taking A Chance
Taking Aim
Taking A Stand
Taking Credit
Taking Notes
Taking Sabbatical
Tale Of Two Cities

Talent Search
Talent Scout
Talent Show
Talisman
Tallahassee
Talk Is Cheap
Talk Nice
Talk Of The Town
Talk Radio
Talk Show Host
Talk The Talk
Tally Ho
Tambourine
Tangier
Tannenbaum
Tanqueray
Tantalizing
Tantalizing Tales
Tap Dancer
Tapestry
Tarot
Tarot Card
Tarzan
Task Master
Task Oriented

Taste Of Texas
Tasty Cake
Tattoo
Tax Break
Tax Cutter
Tax Deduction
Tax Evasion
Tax Free
Taxi Driver
Tax Reduction
Tax Refund
Tax Shelter
Teacher's Aide
Teacher's Note
Tea For Two
Tea Party
Technical Delegate
Technical Difficulty
Technical Jargon
Technical Timing
Teddy Bear
Telepathic
Tell Me True
Tell Me Why
Telltale Sign

Telluride
Temperature's Rising
Tempest
Tempest In A Teapot
Temptation
Tenacious Texan
Tennessee Waltz
Tennis Ace
Tennis Anyone?
Tentative
Tentative Plan
Tequila
Terms Of Agreement
Terms Of Endearment
Terrapin Station
Testify
Testimony
Test Pattern
Test The Waters
Tête À Tête
Texas Destiny
Thank God It's Friday
Thank Goodness
Thanks For The
   Memories

That Certain Charm
That Certain Feeling
That Certain Smile
That Old Feeling
That's A Given
That's A Wrap
That's Debatable
That's Entertainment
That's Final
That's Kharma
That's Typical
Theater Buff
Theater Goer
Theatrical Performer
Then Again
Theory In Action
Theory Of Evolution
There'll Be Talk
Thesaurus
Thesbian
Thick Accent
Thin Air
Thing Of Glory
Things Happen
Thinking Cap

Think Positive
Think Twice
Third Degree
Third Dimension
Third Encore
This End Up
This Is It
This Story Just In
Thoreau
Thought For The Day
Thousands Of
   Promises
Three Act Play
Three Cheers
Three Of A Kind
Three Point Landing
Three Quarter Time
Three Squared
Three's A Charm
Three's A Crowd
Three Sheets To
   The Wind
Three Wishes
Thrill Seeker
Throwing Kisses

Thumbs-Up
Thunder Creek
Thunderbird
Thunder Bolt
Thunder Cloud
Thunderhead
Thunder's Echo
Thurman
Thyme
Tiara
Ticker Tape
Ticket To Ride
Tickle Me Pink
Tickle My Fancy
Tickle Your Fancy
Tic-Tac-Toe
Tidal Wave
Tidbit
Tide Me Over
Tie Breaker
Tie One On
Tight Wad
'Til Kingdom Come
Tilt Wheel
Timbuktu

Time After Time
Time Alone
Time Flies
Time For A Change
Time For Dreaming
Time Goes On
Timeless
Timely Fashion
Timely Manner
Time Machine
Time Marches On
Time On My Hands
Time Out
Time Passage
Timepiece
Time Slips By
Times Square
Times Two
Time Tested
Time Travel
Time Traveler
Time Will Tell
Timex
Time Zone
Tin Pan Alley

Tinsel Tiger
Tinsel Town
Tip Of The Day
Tiptoe Through
    The Tulips
Tiramisu
Tireless
Tis True
Tit For Tat
Title Holder
Titlelist
T.L.C.
To A Different Tune
To A New Level
To Another Level
Toast Of The Town
To A Tee
To Die For
To Each His Own
To Eternity
Toe The Line
To High Heavens
Token Favorite
Told You So
Toledo

Tolleson's Blue
Toll-Free
Tolstoy
Tomorrow At Dawn
Tongue In Cheek
Tongue Twister
Tons Of Fun
Too Cool
Too Expensive
Too Much
Too Much Fun
Tool Time
Tools Of The Trade
Toot Your Horn
Topeka
Topic Of Discussion
Topkapi
Top Of The Line
Top Of The List
Top Secret
Topsy Turvey
Topsider
Top Spin
Torpedo
Torreador

Tosca
Toscano
To Sir With Love
Toss The Dice
Toss-Up
Tostado
Total Commitment
Total Eclipse
Total Effect
Totalitarian
Totally Natural
Totally Neutral
Totally Rad
Total Recall
Total Surprise
To Tell The Truth
To The Bank
To The Contrary
To The Hilt
To The Limit
To The Max
To The Moon
To The Nines
To The Point
To The Top

To The Rescue
To This Day
Touch Base
Touchdown
Touché
Touch Of Dutch
Touch Of Honey
Touch Of Perfection
Touchstone
Touch The Moon
Touch Tone
Toulouse Lautrec
Tour De Force
Tour De France
Tourist Trap
Tournament
Tour Of Duty
Tout Le Monde
Town Car
Town Crier
Town Gambler
Town Gossip
Town Scandal
Townsend
Town Square

Town Squire
Town Talk
To Your Liking
Trademark
Trade Secret
Tradesman
Trade Wind
Trading Card
Trading Places
Tradition
Trafalgar Square
Traffic Control
Traffic Director
Traffic Jam
Traffic Report
Tranquillity
Transcendor
Transient
Transit Authority
Travel Agent
Traveled Abroad
Traveling Minstrel
Traveling Salesman
Treasure Hunt
Trendsetter

Très Bien
Très Chic
Très Intrepid
Très Jolie
Triage
Trial By Jury
Trial Run
Tribunal
Tribune
Trickle Down Theory
Trick Of The Trade
Trigger
Trigger-Nometry
Trigonometry
Trilogy
Trinity
Triple Crown
Triple Sec
Triple Threat
Tripoli
Triumph
Triumphant
Triumphant Spirit
Trivial Pursuit
Trooper

Trophy
Tropical Breeze
Troubadour
Trouble Free
Troubleshooter
Troublesville
Trousseau
Trudeau
True Believer
True Confessions
True Elegance
True Grit
True Illusion
True Lies
True Nature
True Story
True To Form
Truly Lovable
Truly Motivated
Trump
Trump Card
Trust Fund
Trust In Me
Trust Me
Trustworthy

Truth Be Told
Truth Or Consequences
Tryst
Tsunami
Tucson
Tulip
Tulsa
Tumbleweed
Tune-Up
Tunnel Vision
Tunza Talent
Turbo Charged
Turbo Charger
Turning Leaf
Turning Point
Turnkey Operation
Turn Me Loose
Turn Of The Century
Turn Of The Tide
Turn The Key
Turn The Tide
Tuscaloosa
Tuxedo Junction
Twelfth Of Never

Twentieth Century
Twenty Twenty
Twenty-Four Carat
Twice As Good
Twice As Nice
Twilight Blue
Twilight Circus
Twilight Sky
Twilight Time
Twilight Zone
Twisted Plot
Twisted Story
Twist 'N Turns
Twist Of Fate
Two By Four
Two If By Sea
Two Left Feet
Two Pair
Two Part Harmony
Two-Riffic
Two Step
Two Thumbs Up
Two-Timer
Two-Tone
Two To Tango

Typecast
Typical
Typical Situation

U

U2
Ubiquitous Timing
U.F.O.
Ulterior Motive
Ultimate Concern
Ultimate Pleasure
Ultimate Power
Ultimate Proof
Ultimate Weapon
Ultimatum
Ultra
Ultra Cool
Ultra Smart
Ultra Violet
Ultrasuede
Unabridged Version
Unanimous
Unbelievable

Uncanny
Uncanny Ability
Unchained Melody
Uncharted Territory
Unclaimed Treasure
Uncle Sam
UnCola
Uncommon Valor
Unconditional
Unconventional
Undauntable
Undeniable
Underclassman
Under Construction
Under Contract
Undercover
Under Cover Agent
Under Current
Underdressed
Under Full Sail
Under Oath
Under Orders
Under Pressure
Under Protest
Understated

Left: Ardus and Sandy Vogt.
Above: Gregg and Lise Blumenthal.
Both photo contributed by Suzanne Drnec of Chino, CA.

Understatement
Under The Circumstances
Under The Gun
Under The Influence
Under The Mistletoe
Under The Spell
Under The Wire
Under Warranty

Undetermined Amount
Undetermined Influence
Undo Influence
Unemployed
Unethical
Unexpected
Unfinished Symphony
Unfolding Plot
Unforgettable
Uniform Code
Union Dues
Union Member
Unique
Unique Moment
United Way
United We Stand
Universal Donor
Universal Language
Unknown Artist
Unknown Soldier
Unlimited Potential
Unlock The Magic
Unmarked Car

Unorthodox
Unqualified Success
Unquestionable
Unraveling Mystery
Unreal
Unsolved Mystery
Unsung Hero
Unsurpassed
Until Proven Guilty
Until Then
Until Tomorrow
Untold Story
Untouchable
Unused Alibi
Unwritten Law
Up Attitude
Up Beat
Up For Grabs
Up For Renewal
Up For Review
Up Front
Upgrade
Up In Arms
Up In The Air
Up My Sleeve

Upon Reflection
Upper Classman
Upper Crust
Uppercut
Upper Deck
Upper Echelon
Upper Hand
Uppity Snuppity
Upscale
Upstaged
Upstanding Citizen
Up A Creek
Up Tempo
Up To Chance
Up To Date
Up To Me
Up To Mischief
Up To Snuff
Upward Promotion
Up With The Joneses
Uranium
Urban Cowboy
Urban Legend
Urban Renewal
Urgent Business

Suzy. Photo contributed by Trudy Powers of Sebastopol, CA.

Urgent Message
Urge To Splurge
Ursa Major
U.S.A.
U.S. Air
Useful Information
User Friendly
Use Your Imagination
U.S.O.
Usual Suspect
Utilityman
Utmost Attention
Utmost Faith
Utopia

V

Vacation Time
Vagabond
Valedictorian
Valentine
Valerio
Valet Parking
Valiant Successor

Valuable Asset
Value Packed
Vamoose
Vanderbilt
Vandyke
Vanishing Act
Vanishing Breed
Vanity
Vanity Fair
Van Winkle
Varsity Player
Vegas
Velocity
Velour
Velvet
Velvet Derby
Velveteen
Velvet Ribbons
Velvet Tux
Venture Capital
Venture Capitalist
Venus De Milo
Verbatim
Verdict
Vertical Promotion

Vertigo
Very Continental
Very Interesting
Vested Interest
Veteran's Viewpoint
Via Jet
Vicarious
Viceroy
Vice Versa
Vichyossoise
Victorian Era
Victorian Ways
Victorious
Victory
Victory Lap
Viewer's Choice
Viewfinder
Viewing Pleasure
View Master
Viewpoint
Vigilante
Village Voice
Vincenzo
Virtual Reality
Virtuoso

Virtuous
Vis À Vis
Visible Faith
Visible Wind
Visiting Priviledges
Visitor's Rites
Visual Aid
Visual Effects
Visualize That
Vital Information
Vitality
Vital Perfection
Vital Signs
Vital Statistics
Vitamin A
Vitamin Deficient
Viva La Dance
Viva La Difference
Viva Las Vegas
Vivid Imagination
Voo Doo
Voodoo Magic
Voice Mail
Voice Of Authority
Voice Of Command

Voice Of Reason
Voila
Volare
Voltage Regulator
Volunteer
Voluptuous
Vortex
Voulez Vous
Vow Of Silence

W

Wadsworth
Wage Earner
Wait For Me
Wait For The Beep
Waiting In The Wings
Waiting To Exhale
Wake Me When
   It's Over
Wake Up Call
Waldorf
Walkabout
Walkon

Walk On By
Walks The Walk
Walla Walla
Wall Street
Wall Street Demon
Wall Street Tycoon
Wallflower
Wallstreet Blues
Walnut Soup
Waltzing Matilda
Waltzing Rhythm
Waltzing To Ragtime
Wanna Bee
War Bonnet
War Chief
Warlord
Warmest Wishes
Warp Speed
Washington's
   Crossing
Watch Word
Waterford
Waterford Crystal
Watergate
Waterloo

Watermark
Watership Down
Wavelength
Way Back When
Way Out
Way With Words
Wayward Wind
Weatherbee
Weather Forecast
Weather Permitting
Weather Report
Weather The Storm
We Be Jammin'
Web Site
Webster
Wedgwood
Wednesday's Whim
Weekend In L.A.
Weekend Rendezvous
Weekend Warrior
Weekly Allowance
Weeping Willow
Weird Science
Welcome Back
Welcome Home

Welfare Reform
Well Heeled
Wellington
Well-Kept Secret
Wells Fargo
Wellsley
Wembley
We Shall Overcome
Wesley
Westchester
West Coast
Western Union
Westmoreland
West Palm
West Side Story
West Wind
West World
Westerly Wind
Western Breeze
What A Coincidence
What A Concept
What A Deal
What A Jock
What A Lift
What A Sport

Whatever
What If?
What, Me Worry?
What's In A Name
What's My Line?
What's Up Doc?
What's What
Wheaties
Wheel Of A Deal
Wheeler Dealer
When In Time
When It Matters Most
Where It's At
Where There's Truth
Wherewithall
Whimsical
Whippersnapper
Whirlwind
Whiskey Sour
Whisp Of Luck
Whisper
Whisper Hill
Whispering Winds
Whisper Jet
Whisperwind

Whistle In The Dark
Whistle Stop
Whitmore
Who Dunnit
Who Knew
Whole Enchilada
Whoppers
Why Certainly
Why Not?
Why Worry
Wide Angle
Wide Exposure
Wiffenpoof
Wild Applause
Wild Blue Yonder
Wild Card
Wildcat Strike
Wildcatter
Wild Goose Chase
Wild Promises
Wildwood
Will Build To Suit
Willing Partner
Willow
Willowby

Will Power
Wilmington
Winchester
Windfall
Wind Dancer
Windjammer
Window Of
    Opportunity
Window Reflections
Windows Of The Mind
Windows Of The World
Winds Of Change
Windsong
Windsor Castle
Wind Spirit
Windswept
Windwalker
Windy City
Wing And A Prayer
Wing Dinger
Winged Dancer
Wing Tips
Wings Of A Dove
Wings Of Desire
Wings Of Fantasy

Winner
Winner Take All
Winning Combination
Winning Hand
Winning Spirit
Winning Streak
Winning Ticket
Winning Touch
Winning Ways
Winsome
Winston Way
Winterberry
Winter's Wisdom
Winter Weather
Winterwood
Winthrop's Way
Win-Win Situation
Wired For Sound
Wire To Wire
Wise Warrior
Wishbone
Wishful Thinking
Wish I May
Wish I Might
Wishing Well

Barnum and Olivia Galvin. Photo contributed by Catherine Lewis of Petaluma, CA.

Kiamichi Rooster. Photo contributed by Nanci Falley & Leana Westergaard, American Indian Horse Registry of Lockhart, TX.

Wish Me Luck
Wish Me Well
Wisteria
Witching Hour
With All Due Respect
With Baited Breath
With Bells On
With Certainty
With Dignity
With Due Respect
With Gratitude
With Gusto
Withholding Evidence
With Honor
With Honors
Within Reason
Within The Law
With Interest
With Open Arms
Without A Doubt
Without Limits
Without Regret
Without Shame
Without Warning
With Pride

With Regard
With Rhythm
With The Program
Witness For The
  Prosecution
Witness Protection
Witness Testimony
Wizard
Wolfgang
Wonderful Times
Wonderful World
Wonders Never
  Cease
Wonder Years
Won Me Over
Wooden Nickel
Wooden Soldier
Woodstock
Woodwind
Wooly Bully
Word Of Advice
Word Of Honor
Word Of The Day
Word Of Warning
Word On The Street

Word Perfect
Words Of Wisdom
Word To The Wise
Workaholic
Workflow
Working Order
Work In Progress
Work Of Art
World Affairs
World Class
World Leader
World News
World Of Difference
World Traveler
Worth A Glance
Worth The Effort
Worth The Risk
Worth The Wait
Worth Your While
Worthwhile
Worthy Cause
Wrangler
Wrinkle In Time
Writing On The Wall
Written In Stone

Wunderkind
Wilie Coyote
WWW.
WWW.COM

X-Act
Xanadu
Xavier
X-Cel
Xenophen
Xenophobic
Xerox Copy
X X O O
X-Press Mail
X-Rated
X-Ray

Y

Yachtsman
Yada Yada
Yahoo

Yahtzee
Yakety Yak
Yaley
Yankee Candle
Yankee Clipper
Yankee Doodle
Yankee Doodle Dandy
Yankee Pride
Yankee Soldier
Yearning Desire
Yes Indeed
Yes Ma'am
Yes Man
Yessiree
Yesterday
Yesterday's Promise
Yikety Yak
Yonder Mate
Young At Heart
Young
   Whippersnapper
Your Highness
Your Honor
Your Majesty
Your Move

Your Place
Your's Truly
Your Wish Has
   Been Granted
You've Got Mail
You Wish!
Yo Yo
Yucatan
Yule Never Know
Yule Tide
Yum Yum
Yuppie Tendencies

Zany Character
Zap
Zealot
Zealous
Zen Insight
Zenith
Zephyr
Zepplin
Zero Defects

Zero Gravity
Zero Hour
Zero In On
Ziegler
Zigger
Zig-Zag
Zillion Laughs
Zillions Of Promises
Zinger
Zionist
Zip
Zip Code
Zipper
Zodiac
Zoloft
Zombie
Zoom
Zucchini

*Bentley (the horse) and Butch. Photo contributed by
the Appaloosa Horse Club of Moscow, ID.*

NAMES BEGINNING WITH "THE"

The Accountant
The Accused
The Acrobat
The Admiral
The Advance Man
The Advocate
The Alien
The All American
The Amazon
The Ambassador
The Analyst
The Answer Man
The Apprentice
The Aristocrat
The Artisan
The Attorney
The Auditor
The Author
The Bailiff
The Ballerina
The Band-Wagon
The Bandit

The Barber Of Seville
The Barfly
The Baron
The Baroness
The Bartender
The Beach Bunny
The Beachcomber
The Beat Goes On
The Bellboy
The Bellhop
The Best For Last
The Best Of Both
    Worlds
The Best Of Times
The Best Part
The Better Half
The Big Picture
The Big Time
The Bionic Woman
The Bishop
The Bohemian
The Bondsman

The Border Guard
The Boss
The Boss' Daughter
The Bouncer
The Bounty Hunter
The Boxer
The Boy Friend
The Boy In Blue
The Bridegroom
The Buck Stops Here
The Butler
The Butler Did It
The Cable Guy
The Cadet
The Camera Man
The Candidate
The Capilalist
The Cardinal
The Cartel Boss
The Catalyst
The Cat's Pajamas
The Cat's Meow

The Celebrity
The Centurion
The C.E.O.
The Challenger
The Chameleon
The Chancellor
The Changeling
The Chaperon
The Charmer
The Chauffeur
The Cheerleader
The Chief Justice
The Choreogapher
The Chronicle
The Cincinnati Kid
The Cisco Kid
The Client
The Clone
The Co-Defendant
The Colonel
The Comet
The Commissioner

The Confederate
The Conjurer
The Conquering Hero
The Consultant
The Contender
The Contessa
The Contestant
The Conversation Piece
The Councilman
The Count
The Countess
The Country Doctor
The Crusader
The Cure
The Customer
The Cutting Edge
The Cyclone
The Cynic
The D.A.
The Dark Side
The Debutante
The Delegate
The Deliveryman

The Detective
The Dilettante
The Diplomat
The Director
The Distinguished Gentleman
The Domino Theory
The Drill Sargent
The Duke
The Dutchess
The Echo
The Edge Of Night
The Editor
The Eleventh Hour
The Embezzler
The Emperor
The End Of Time
The Endowment
The Energizer
The English Patient
The Entertainer
The Epitome
The Eraser
The Establishment
The Evangelist

The Eyes Have It
The Executive
The Expert
The Fact Is
The Fair Sex
The Favorite
The Federalman
The Firm
The Fittest Survivor
The Flatterer
The Flirt
The Force
The Foreigner
The Fortune Hunter
The Freelancer
The Freshman
The Fugitive
The Fullback
The Gambler
The General
The Genius
The Genuine Article
The Gist Of It
The Gladiator
The Globetrotter

The Go-Between
The Godfather
The Goodbye Girl
The Good Samaritan
The Governor
The Gravy Train
The Great Cover-Up
The Great Gatsby
The Great Pretender
The Guitarist
The Hacker
The Handyman
The Happening
The Hard Way
The Head Coach
The Headliner
The Heir
The Heiress
The Hermit
The Heroine
The Highlander
The Hit Man
The Hobbit
The Hobo
The Hooligan

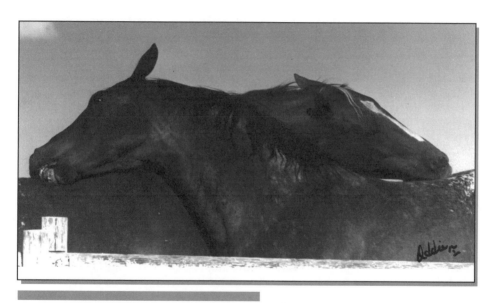

Lullaby (left) and Pixie. Photo by Lenora Oddie of Alberta, Canada.
Photo contributed by the Appaloosa Horse Club of Moscow, ID.

The Hope Diamond
The Huckster
The Hustler
The Iceman Cometh
The Immigrant
The Impersonator
The In Crowd
The Informer
The Inheritance
The Inkspot
The Innovator
The Intellectual
The Interloper
The Interpreter
The Investigator
The Irishman
The Irony Of It
The Jewel
The Joker
The Journalist
The Judge
The Juror
The Jury's Out
The Landlady

The Landlord
The Last Detail
The Last Hurrah
The Last Word
The Leading Edge
The Learning Curve
The Legacy
The Legend
The Librarian
The Line Of Fire
The Living End
The Logo
The Look
The Magician
The Magistrate
The Mailman
The Main Event
The Man
The Marlboro Man
The Matador
The Matriarch
The Mayor
The Mentor
The Mercenary
The Mermaid

The Midas Touch
The Middleman
The Mikado
The Milkman Delivers
The Milky Way
The Missionary
The Moment
The Monarch
The More, The Merrier
The Musician
The Music Man
The Myth
The Navigator
The Neighs Have It
The New Deal
The Newsmaker
The New Yorker
The Novelist
The Nth Degree
The Nutty Professor
The Observer
The Obvious Choice
The One And Only
The Only One
The Optimist

The Organizer
The Other Side
The Other Side Of
   Midnite
The Other Woman
The Outlaw
The Overseer
The Palace Guard
The Paralegal
The Patriarch
The Patriot
The Peacemaker
The Perfectionist
The "Perp"
The Perpetrator
The Philanthropist
The Plot Thickens
The Poet
The Preacher's Wife
The President
The Price Is Right
The Princess
The Princess In The
   Tower
The Prize Fighter

The Procrastinator
The Professional
The Professor
The Promise
The Prophet
The Prosecutor
The Proxy
The Publisher
The Pulitzer Prize
The Quarterback
The Quiet Man
The Realist
The Real McCoy
The Real Thing
The Rebel
The Republican
The Renegade
The Replacement
The Repo Man
The Reporter
The Representative
The Right Stuff
The Right Thing
The Right Touch
The Ringleader

The Riot Act
The Ritz
The Rogue
The Rookie
The Rose
The Saint
The Sales Associate
The Sand Man
The Scene Stealer
The Scholar
The Scope Of Things
The Scoundrel
The Search Is On
The Search Is Over
The Secret's Out
The Seeker
The Settlement
The Shadow
The Showstopper
The Shuffler
The Skeptic
The Snow Queen
The Soaps
The Soldier
The Solution

The Sorcerer
The Squire
The Stamp Of
  Approval
The Stand-In
The Statesman
The Statistician
The Stowaway
The Substitute
The Suitor
The Supervisor
The Tailor
The Taxman
The Team Leader
The Technician
The Tempest
The Temptress
The Terminator
The Thinker
The Tie That Binds
The Tin Man
The Troubadour
The Troublemaker
The Truth Machine
The Tutor

The Tycoon
The Ultimate
The Undersigned
The Verdict's In
The Villain
The Virtuoso
The Visionary
The Voice In My Head
The Voyager
The Wanderer
The War Lord
The Warrior
The Wave
The Wave Of The
  Future
The Weatherman
The Welter Weight
The White Sox
The Whiz Kid
The Wiseman
The Witching Hour
The Witness
The Wizard
The Word Is Out
The Wordsmith

97

Pregnant Pom Pom. Photo contributed by Dawn Lyons of Montogmery, NY.

FILLIES & MARES

Acapella
Abbey Road
Ain't She Sweet
Alice In Wonderland
All About Eve
Allison's Alibi
All The Glory
Alluring Female
Always The
  Bridesmaid
Amaryllis
Amazing Grace
Amazon Woman
Amelia Bedelia
American Girl
An Article Of Faith
Anastasia
A Natural Blond
Angelique
Animated Alyce
Anna Banana
Annabelle Lee
Ann Arbor

Annie Hall
Annie Oakley
Antoinette
Aphrodite
Avon Lady
Baby Ruth
Bahama Mama
Ballerina
Ballerina Magic
Barbarella
Barbie Doll
Barb Wire
Bar Maid
Beauty Queen
Bella Donna
Bella Mia
Bella Vista
Belle Of The Ball
Best Supporting
  Actress
Betsy Ross
Betty Boop
Betty Crocker

Between Us Girls
Big Bertha
Bit Of Honey
Black Eyed Susan
Blondie
Blue Belle
Blue Jean
Blue Nun
Blue Rose
Bobby's Girl
Bonnie Bell
Bonnie Blue
Bonnie Prospect
Boss Lady
Boy Crazy
Break Of Dawn
Bridget Bardot
Brook Lynn
Brown Betty
Brown-Eyed Girl
Bunny Hop
Burgundy Lace
Busy Bee

Cactus Flower
Cajun Queen
Calamity Jane
California Girl
Call To Glory
Camellia
Cameo
Camille
Campus Queen
Candide
Candy Cane
Candygram
Cape May
Career Girl
Carrie A Tune
Carrie Nation
Centerfold
Chantilly Lace
Chantilly Lady
Charlotte's Web
Chatty Cathy
Cheerleader
Cherokee Princess

Chili Millie
China Doll
Choir Girl
Christmas Carol
Cinderella
Cinnamon Girl
City Flirt
City Girl
Claire DeLune
Clandestine
Classy Lady
Clover
Coal Miner's
   Daughter
Copper Penny
Cotton Candy
Country Girl
Cover Girl
Cowgirl
Cristabelle
Crown Victoria
Curly Sue
Custom Maid
Cynical Cissie

Daddy's Girl
Daisy Chain
Daisy Mae
Damsel In Distress
Dancing Matilda
Dancing Nancy
Dance 'Til Dawn
Dawn Patrol
Dawn's Early Light
Day Lily
Dear Abby
Debutante
Debutante Dame
Debutante Lady
Debutante Miss
Delilah
Delta Dawn
Desdemona
Designing Woman
Desiree
Devil In A Blue Dress
Diamond Lil
Dilithium Crystal
Divine Grace
Dixie Belle

Dizzy Miss Lizzy
Dolly Lama
Dragon Lady
Dream Of Glory
Dresden China
Driving Miss Daisy
Duchess Of York
Dutch Girl
Educating Rita
Eleanor Rigby
Electra
Electric Ladyland
Elvira
Enchanted Lady
English Penny
Enticing Lady
Estée Lauder
Eureka
Fajita
Fall From Grace
Fannie Mae
Farina
Fashion Belle
Fat Lady Sings
Femme Fatale

Felicity
First Lady
Flaming Frieda
Fleur-De-Lis
Flirt
Flo Jo
Flower Child
Flower Power
Foxy Lady
Fraulien
French Lace
French Twist
Fresh As A Daisy
Fuchsia
Funny Girl
Funny Lady
G.I. Jane
Gabrielle
Gaelic Girl
Garbo
Geez Louise
Geisha Girl
Genie In A Bottle
Georgia On My Mind
Georgia Peach

Gibson Girl
Girl's Best Friend
Ghetto Girl
Gidget
Gigi
Ginger
Ginnie Mae
Girl Friday
Girl Next Door
Girl Scout
Giselle
Glory Be
Glory Days
Good Faith
Good Golly Miss
  Molly
Goodnight Irene
Goodnight
  Mrs. Calabash
Great Garbo
Griselda
Guinevere
Gypsy Rose Lee
Gypsy Woman
Hail Mary

Harriet The Spy
Hazelnut
Hat Check Girl
Heavens To Betsy
Heidi
Hello Dolly
Help Me Rhonda
Helpful Hannah
Helpful Harriet
Her Majesty
Hey Jude
Holly Go Lightly
Homecoming Queen
Honeybee
Honey Be Good
Honey Brown
Honey Bunch
Honeycomb
Honeydew
Honeysuckle
Honeysuckle Rose
Honky Tonk Woman
Hootchy Kootchy
  Mama
Hosanna

Hot Flash
Hurricane Edna
Hurricane Eleanor
I Love Lucy
Ima Showoff
Imperial Girl
Imperial Lady
Indiana Joan
Indian Princess
Indigo Girl
Irish Lace

Iron Maiden
Isadora
It's A Girl Thing
Jacinda
Jane's Addiction
Jezebel
Joan Of Arc
Joy Forever
Joy Ride
Joy To The World
Judy, Judy, Judy
Jumanji

*Antama Pasha with 5-day-old filly, Mabrouk Ansar.
Photo contributed by International Arabian Horse Registry
of North America of Marysville, OH.*

Jump For Joy
Just Sue
Katy Did
Kept Woman
Kewpie Doll
Kiss Me Kate
Kitty Hawk
K-k-k-katie
Lady
Lady Bird
Lady Boss
Lady Bountiful
Lady Bug
Lady Chatterly
Lady Clairol
Lady Doctor
Lady Eve
Lady Godiva
Lady Guinevere
Lady In Waiting
Lady Jane
Ladylike
Lady Luck
Lady Of Spain

Lady Of The House
Lady's Choice
Lady's First
Lady's Night
Lady Soul
Lara's Theme
Last Rose Of
    Summer
Laura Ashley
Lazy Susan
Leading Lady
Liberated Lady
Liberty Belle
Lily Of The Valley
Little Darling
Little Mary Sunshine
Little Match Girl
Little Miss Fit
Little Miss Muffet
Little Princess
Local Girl Makes
    Good
Lois Lane
Lola
Lonely Girl

Long Tall Sally
Lorna Doone
Lover Girl
Lucille Says
Lucinda's Blue
    Bonnet
Luck Be A Lady
Lucy Goosey
Lucy In The Sky
Luscious
Ma Belle
Madame Bovary
Madame Butterfly
Madame Secretary
Madcap Heiress
Madeline
Madonna
Mafia Princess
Maggie May
Maggie Now
Magic Lady
Maiden Voyage
Maid In America
Maid Marion
Maid Of Honor

Maid The Cut
Maid To Order
Mail Order Bride
Majestic Lady
Margaritaville
Margarita
Marie Antoinette
Marigold
Marilyn Monroe
Marimba
Mama-San
Marnie
Martha's Vineyard
Mary Go Round
Mary Jane
Mary Poppins
Material Girl
Mateus Rose
Maybelline
Meddlesome
Melancholy Baby
Melody
Memphis Belle
Merry
Merry Lady

Merry Widow
Mesopotamian
    Princess
Meter Maid
Mighty Aphrodite
Millennia
Minerva
Minnie-Apolis
Minnie Mouse
Minnie Pearl
Minuette
Miranda's Rights
Miss Adventure
Miss America
Miss American Pie
Miss Begotten
Miss Behavin'
Miss Chevious
Miss Chief
Miss Conduct
Miss Congeniality
Miss Daisy
Miss Demeanor
Miss Ellaneous
Miss Fit

Miss Garbo
Miss Goodie Two
    Shoes
Miss Informed
Miss Know It All
Miss Manners
Miss Marple
Miss Prim
Miss Print
Miss Priss
Miss Saigon
Miss Snapdragon
Miss Understood
Miss Universe
Molly Brown
Moment Of Glory
Mona Lisa
Moon Goddess
Morning Glory
Mother Jones
Mrs. Miniver
Mrs. Wiggins
Mustang Sally
My Darling
    Clementine

My Fair Lady
My Gal Sal
My Girl
Natasha
National Velvet
Native Rose
Naughty Girl
Nellie Bly
Novella
Oh Mama
Old Maid
Olive Oil
Olympia
One Perfect Rose
Oops A Daisy
Operetta
Ophelia
Oprah
Orphan Annie
Pandora
Paper Roses
Party Girl
Paths Of Glory
Peak Of Dawn
Pearl Harbor

Pearls Of Wisdom
Peg O' My Heart
Pennies From Heaven
Penny Ante
Penny Candy
Penny Farthing
Penny Lane
Pennywise
Peoria
Peppermint Patty
Perils Of Pauline
Persephone
Personal Secretary
Petticoat
Piña Colada
Pin-Up Girl
Pippi Longstocking
Plain Jane
Play Misty For Me
Playgirl
Poison Ivy
Polka Dot
Pollyanna
Polygraph Test
Portrait Of A Lady

103

Proud Mary
Pretty As A Picture
Pretty As You Please
Pretty In Pink
Pretty Woman
Prima Ballerina

Prima Donna
Princess Di
Princess Grace
Princess Leah
Princess In A Pickle
Prissy Miss
Prom Queen
Proud Mary
Prudence
Queen Anne's Lace
Queen Bee

Queen Bess
Queen For A Day
Queen Of Hearts
Queen Of Sorcery
Queen Of The Nile
Queen's Command
Queen's Quest
Quiche Lorraine
Rag Doll
Raggedy Ann
Rainy Day Woman
Ramblin' Rose
Rapunzel
Red Hot Mama
Riannon
Ride, Sally Ride
Ring Around The
    Rosie
Ritzy Lady
Road To Glory
Rose Garden
Rose Glow
Rose Of Sharon
Rose Petal
Rosebud

Rosetta Stone
Rosie O'Grady
Rosy Outlook
Run-Around Sue
Sadie Hawkins
Saint Patty
Santa Barbara
Sarah Plain And Tall
Sara Lee
Sassy
Savannah Smiles
Saving Grace
Say Grace
Scarlet O'Hara
Secret Sister
Seeking Susan
Serenity
Shades Of Grace
Shady Lady
Shalimar
Shantytown Girl
She-Devil
Sheer Joy
She's A Pepper
She's So Vain

Mary Ellen. Photo contributed by June V. Evers of Goshen, NY.

Weebok. Photo contributed by M. Williams, International Generic Horse Association of Rancho Palos Verdes, CA.

She's The One
Shim Shim Sherree
Shy Girl
Shy Violet
Sister Sister
Sleigh Belle
Slick Chick
Slick Tracy
Smalltown Girl
Snow Queen
Snow White
Sob Sister
Social Grace
Socialite
Song Of Bernadette
Sophisticated Lady
Soprano
Sorceress
Sorority Sister
So Sue Me
Southern Belle
Southern Miss
Southside Sally
Spelling Bee
Spice Girl

Stable Mabel
St. Pauli Girl
Stella Doro
Stormin' Red Hot
    Mama
String Of Pearls
Stubborn Miss
Stunning
Suddenly Susan
Sugar Magnolia
Sugar-Plum
Sugar-Plum Fairy
Sugartime
Sunflower Sue
Surfer Girl
Susie Q
Swanky Lady
Sweet Adelaide
Sweet Adeline
Sweet As Sugar
Sweet Caroline
Sweet Charity
Sweet Georgia
    Brown
Sweet Petunia

Sweet Sue
Swiss Miss
Tabitha's Secret
Tabby Cat
Taco Belle
Tallahassee
Taste Of Honey
Teen Angel
Teenie Bopper
Ten Penny Nail
Texas Scarlet
That Girl
Tiger Lily
Tinker Bell
Tin Lizzie
Tomboy
Topeka
Town Flirt
Tulsa
Twisted Sister
Ukelele Lola
Unladylike
Up Before Dawn
Upsy Daisy
Uptown Girl

Valley Girl
Velvet Rose
Victoria Secret
Viking Princess
Violet Sky
Virginia Slim
Waltzing Matilda
Westminster Abby
What's Her Name
Whistling Dixie
Wichita
Wilma
Witch Hazel
Witch Hunt
Witchy Woman
With Social Graces
Woman Of
    Substance
Woman's Intuition
Working Girl
Yukon Belle

Left: Chakola's Calgary. Photo contributed by Jane E. Scott, the Cleveland Bay Horse Society of South Windham, CT. Above: Sabino. Photo contributed by Darrell Dodds, American Paint Horse Association of Fort Worth, TX.

COLTS, GELDINGS & STALLIONS

Absent-Minded
Professor
According To Hoyle
Action Jackson
Adam's Rib
Adonis
Air Bud
Air Jordan
Aladdin
Alias Alfred
Allegro
A Man About Town
A Man For All
Seasons
A Man's Man
American Flyer
Andy Capp
An Ordinary Man
Apollo
Art Deco
Artemis
Art Nouveau
A Self-Made Man

Ask Jake
Athletico
Atlas Shrugged
Atta Boy
At Will
Axel Foley
Bachelor Of Art
Bad Boy
Barnaby
Barnacle Bill
Bartholomew
Bartleby
Barton
Bashful Bob
Basil
Batman
Baxter
Baylor
Beau Geste
Beaumont
Belvedere
Bench Mark
Ben Hur

Bentley
Big Brother
Bill Board
Bill Of Rights
Bill Of Sale
Billy Bud
Billy Joe Bob
Blue Boy
Blues Brother
Bobby Sox
Bogart
Bojangles
Booker T.
Boy George
Boy Oh Boy
Boy Wonder
Brian's Song
Broadway Joe
Bronco Bill
Brooks Brother
Buckaroo
Buckley
Budd Light

Bud Wiser
Buffalo Bill
Bugle Boy
Bugsy Malone
Burke's Law
Buster Brown
Byron
Call Me Charlie
Candy Man
Candyman Can
Capote
Captain Courageous
Captain Hook
Captain Marvel
Captain Midnight
Carmichael
Casanova
Casey's Shadow
Catch Some Rays
Charles Dickens
Charlestown
Charlie Brown
Charlie Chaplin

Colts, Geldings & Stallions

Charlie Daniel's Band
Chase Manhattan
Cheyenne
Chief Rebel
Chip Off The Old Block
Choir Boy
Chopin
Chris Craft
Christopher Robin
Churchill
Cisco Kid
Citizen Kane
Clark Bar
Clark Gable
Cliffhanger
Cliff Notes
Cody
College Boy
Columbo
Columbus
Commander Cody
Commander In Chief
Company Man

Confidence Man
Confucius
Cool Hand Luke
Co-Pilot
Copperfield
Cosmic Cowboy
Cosmic Ray
Cosmo
Cosmopolitan Gentleman
Country Boy
Country Squire
Cowboy's Dust
Crimson King
Cross Beau
Crown Prince
Culligan Man
Curious George
CY Young
Daddy Warbucks
Dance With Me Henry
Daniel Boone
Danny Boy
Dante

Dante's Peak
Dapper Dan
D'Artagnon
Da Vinci
Davis Cup
Davy Crockett
Dean's List
Dear John
Dear Sir
DeGaulle
Degas
Demetrious
Deuteronomy
Diamond Jim
Dicaprio
Dick Tracy
Dilbert
Dirty Harry
Dominique
Dom Perignon
Don Juan
Doubting Thomas
Dow Jones
Dr. Doolittle
Dr. Kildaire

Dr. Livingston
Dr. No
Dr. Pepper
Dr. Seusse
Dr. Spock
Dreamboat
Dream Lad
Drummer Boy
Duke It Out
Duke Of Earl
Duke Of Windsor
Duncan
Dutch Lad
Earl The Pearl
Edison
Einstein
Electric Cowboy
Elijah Blue
Elmer Fudd
Elmer Gantry
Elvis Lives
Emmett Kelly
Errol Flynn
Even Steven
Fabian

Fair-Haired Boy
Family Jules
Family Man
Famous Amos
Fancy Dan
Farmer Joe
Father Figure
Father Murphy
Father Time
Faulkner
Featuring Fred
Feet Of Clay
Felix
Ferris Bueller
Fibber McGee
Field Marshall
Figaro
Filthy Rich
Finnigan's Rainbow
Fisher King
Fit For A King
Five Star General
Flash Gordon
Fleetwood Mac
Flim Flam Man

For Pete's Sake
Forrest Gump
Frankly Speaking
Freddy Or Not
Fred's Folly
Free Will
Free Willy
Fresh Prince
Friar Tuck
Friendly Lad
For Art's Sake
Four-Star General
Galileo
Gambling Man
Gameboy
Gandolf
Gaylord
General Patton
Gentle Ben
Gentleman Jim
Gentleman Like
Gentlemanly
Gentlemen's
   Agreement
Gentleman's Bet

Gentleman's
   Quarterly
Georgie Boy
Georgie Porgie
Georgio
Geronimo
Gingerbread Man
Givenchy
Goliath
Goodfella
Good Guy
Good Will
Gorgeous George
Gretzky
Gulliver
Gunga Din
Hale Bop
Hamlet
Handsome Devil
Handsome Dude
Hanky Panky
Hans Brinker
Harley Davidson
Harper's Ferry
Harris Tweed

Heartbreak Kid
Heir Apparent
Hemingway
Henry's Garnet
Henry VIII
Hercules
Here's Johnny
High Jack
Highway Robber
Hill Billy
Hilton
Himself The Elf
His Honor
Hit The Jackpot
Hobson's Choice
Homer
Honest Abe
Hopalong Cassidy
Houdini
Howard's End
Huckleberry Finn
Humphrey Bogart
Hurdy Gurdy Man
Hurricane Andrew
Ice Cream Man

109

Colts, Geldings & Stallions

Il Primo
Imperial Lad
Indiana Jones
Indian Joe
In Like Flynn
Inspector Clouseau
Inspector Muldoone
Iron Will
Isaiah's Prophecy
Ivan The Great

Captain Marvel. Photo contributed by Catherine Lewis of Petaluma, CA.

Ivanhoe
Jack Be Nimble
Jack Be Quick
Jack Daniels
Jack Flash
Jack Frost
Jack Of All Trades
Jack Of Diamonds
Jack Of Hearts
Jackpot
Jackson
Jacks Or Better
Jacksonville
Jacob's Ladder
Jacques Cousteau
James Bond
James Dean
Jameson
Jasper
Jefferson
Jehosephet
Jeremiah
Jericho
Jesse James
Jim Bean

Jim Dandy
Jiminy Cricket
Joe Cool
Joe Fashion
Johnny Be Good
Johnny Come Lately
Johnny-On-The-Spot
Johnny Walker
Jolly Roger
Joshua
Journeyman
"Juan" In A Million
"Juan" Of These
   Days
Jumping Jack
Jumping Jack Flash
Jumping Jehosaphat
Jungle George
Jungle Jim
Just Another Gigolo
Kermit
Killjoy
Kilroy Is Here
King Cole
King Lear

King Midas
King Of Hearts
King Of Prussia
King Of The Hill
King Of The
   Mountain
King Of The Road
Kingpin
King's Caper
Kingsized
King's Dominion
King's Manner
King Tut
King Wenceslas
Kipling
Kismet
Kodiak Jack
Kokomo Jo
Kris Kringle
Krushchev
Ladykiller
Lady's Man
Lake George
Laughing Boy
Leading Man

Led Zeppelin
Leroy Brown
Letterman
Liberace
Lieutenant Colonel
Life Of Riley
Like A Gentleman
Likely Lad
Lincoln
Local Boy
Local Hero
Logan
Logan's Run
Lonely Boy
Lonely Lad
Looking For Richard
Looks For Luke
Lord Of The Manor
Lothario
Lover Boy
Lucky Strike
Lucky Lad
Ludwig
Lumber Jack
MacArthur

MacBeth
Machiavelli
Macho Man
Mack The Knife
Macmillan
Macnamara
Mad Max
Magellan
Magnificent
    Amberson
Magnum P.I.
Majestic Prince
Majestic Warrior
Major Klondike
Major League
Major Tom
Make My Day
Mama's Boy
Mandrake
Man In The Moon
Man Of Action
Man Of Fortune
Man Of His Word
Man Of Importance
Man Of La Mancha

Man Of Means
Man Of The Hour
Marathon Man
Marc Antony
Mark My Word
Mark Of Distinction
Mark Of Honor
Marksman
Marquis De Sade
Martial Arts
Masked Man
Master Charge
Master Of Disguise
Master Of Suspense
Master Of The
    Universe
Matisse
Matlock
Matthew
Max A. Millionaire
Maxim
Maximilian
Maxwell Smart
Maxxed Out
Measure Of A Man

Medicine Man
Merlin
Messenger Boy
Michaelangelo
Mickey D.
Middleman
Mighty Casey
Mighty Joe Young
Mighty Max
Mighty Quinn
Mikey Likes It
Miles Standish
Military Man
Missile Man
Mister Boo Boo
Mister McGoo
Mister Peepers
Mister Roberts
Mohawk
Mohican
Monarch
Mon Oncle
Montgomery
Morse Code
Mountain Man

Colts, Geldings & Stallions

Mozart
Mr. Bojangles
Mr. Clean
Mr. Cool
Mr. Curious
Mr. Debonair
Mr. Ed
Mr. Excitement
Mr. Goodbar
Mr. Green Jeans
Mr. Magoo
Mr. Peabody
Mr. President
Mr. Reliable
Mr. Right
Mr. Rogers
Mr. Sandman
Mr. Senator
Mr. Wizard
Mr. Wonderful
Muffin Man
Music Man
My Chauffeur
My Cousin Vinnie

My Guy
My Hero
Mysterious Man
Mystery Man
Napoleon
Native Son
Neon Leon
Newsboy
Nick Of Time
Noble Caesar
Nostradamus
No Way José
Number One Son
Obediah
Odd Man Out
Ogler
O' Henry
Oliver Cromwell
Oliver Twist
One Man Show
Original Art
Oscar Meyer
Othello
Pablo
Pal Joey

Pavarotti
Peeping Tom
Perfect Gentleman
Perfectly Frank
Peterbuilt
Peter Pan
Peter, Peter Pumpkin
    Eater
Peter Piper
Peters Principle
Pharoh Prince
Piano Man
Picasso
Pied Piper
Pillsbury Doughboy
Pink Floyd
Pistol Pete
Plato
Playbill
Playboy
Play It Again Sam
Poetry Man
Poncho
Poor Boy
Pop Art

Port Charles
Port O Prince
Poster Boy
Precious Fellow
Prince Albert
Prince Charles
Prince Charming
Prince Of Bellaire
Prince Of Thieves
Prince Of Wales
Prince Of Windsor
Prince Rainier
Prince Valiant
Printer's Mark
Priority Male
Prisoner # 001
Prisoner Of Zenda
Prodigal Son
Punctuation Mark
Quasimodo
Quiet Man
Quincy
Quite A Guy
Quite Frankly
Quotation Mark

Raisin' Cain
Rambling Man
Rambo
Rambunctious Lad
Ranger Rick
Rayban
Ray Of Hope
Ray Of Light
Ready For Freddy
Regal Rover
Regarding Henry
Rembrandt
Remington
Remy Martin
Renoir
Reubens
Rhett Butler
Rhinestone Cowboy
Richie Rich
Right Hand Man
Ringo
Rip Van Winkle
Robinson Crusoe
Robert's Rule
Rob Roy

Rock-A-Billy
Rocketman
Rocket Scientist
Rockin' Robin
Rock Of Ages
Rock Solid
Rock The Boat
Rocky Balboa
Rocky Road
Roosevelt
Rothschild
Roy Rogers
Rubberband Man
Rudy Valentino
Rumpelstiltskin
Russian Prince
Rusty Nail
Sailor Man
Sam-I-Am
Samson
Sand Man
Sargent Major
Scott Free
Sebastian
Secret Agent Man

Señor Lopez
Seventh Son
Sgt. Pepper
Shakespeare
Shamu
Sheik
Shenandoah
Sherlock
Sherman Tank
Shoeless Joe
Shout About Sam
Silent Sam
Silly Willy
Simon Says
Sinbad
Single Guy
Sir Gallahad
Sir Lancelot
Sir Laugh-A-Lot
Sir Raleigh
Sir Walter
Ski Bum
Skyhawk
Sky King
Skylar

Sloppy Joe
Smart Aleck
Sneaky Pete
Snooty Rudy
Snuffy Smith
Socrates
Solomon
Son Of A Gun
Soul Man
Southern Gent
Spare The Rod
Sparticus
Spiderman
Spinner
Stagedoor Johnny
Stand Up Guy
Stanley Steamer
Stan The Man
Steady Freddy
Steamboat Willie
Steppenwolf
Stingray
Stonewall Jackson
Stormin' Norman
Stormy Knight

113

Colts, Geldings & Stallions

St. Patrick
Straight Man
Strike It Rich
Student Prince
Sugar Daddy
Sugar Ray
Super Bill
Superman
Sweet Talking Guy
Takeover Man
Talisman
Tall, Dark And
 Handsome
Tambourine Man
Tap Mac
Taylor Made
Ted E. Bear
Teen Idol
Test Pilot
That Boy
The King Is Back
Think Rich
Third Man
This Bud's For You

Tiberius
Tim Buck Too!
Tiny Tim
Toe The Mark
Tom Foolery
Tommy Boy
Tommy Gun
Tommy Hawk
Tommy Tucker
Tommy Tuneful
Tom Sawyer
Tom Thumb
To The Max
Toucan Sam
Trademark
Travelin' Man
Tricky Dick
Tricky Ricky
Tron
Trooper
Tucker
Tugboat Tommie
Tyrone Power
Tyson's Corner
Ulysses

Uncle Albert
Union Jack
Urban Cowboy
Valdez
Valentino
Van Dyke
Van Gogh
Vivaldi
Walkaway Joe
Water Mark
W. C. Fields
Welcome Mat
What About Bob?
What A Guy
Wichita Lineman
Wild Bill
Willard
Willful
William Penn
William Tell
Willie Wonka
Will O' Wisp
Willow John
Will Rodgers
Willy Be Good

Willy Nilly
Winston
Winston Churchill
Winter King
Wise Guy
Wizard Of Oz
Wolfman Jack
Wyatt Earp
Wyeth
Yes Man
Yes Sir
Yosemite Sam
Your Average Joe
Yukon Jack
Zachery
Zany Zack
Zeke
Zeus
Zorba
Zorro

PONIES & SMALL HORSES

Alfalfa Sprout
Almond Joy
And Everything Nice
And Puppy Dog Tails
Animal Crackers
Applebee
Apple Jacks
A Real Q.T.
Awesome Blossom
Babar
Baby Rug
Baby Cakes
Baby Ruth
Bachelor Buttons
Bamboozle
Bangles
Banjo
Barney
Bazooka
Bean Sprout
Beau Brummel
Bed Bug

Belly Button
Best Friends
Beetle Juice
Billy The Kid
Bingo
Binkee
Birthday Surprise
Bite Sized
Bit By Bit
Bit Dancer
Bit Of A Brat
Bit Of Magic
Bit Of Welcome
Bit Part
Blindman's Bluff
Blinkey
Blitzen
Bloomers
Bon Bon
Booby Prize
Boomerang
Boston's Baked Bean

Brussel Sprout
Bubble Gum
Buckeroo Bonsai
Buckle My Shoe
Buckwheat
Buff Puff
Bugaboo
Bumble Bee
Bunny Hop
Campfire Girl
Candied Apple
Candy Coated
Candy Kiss
Captain Crunch
Captain Kangaroo
Carousel Ride
Cat's Meow
Chasing Rainbows
Chattanooga Choo
   Choo
Cheerios
Chicklet

Child Prodigy
Child's Play
Chop "Stix"
Cinders
Cisco Kidd
Cocopuff
Confetti
Cookie Cutter
Cookie Monster

Casino. Photo contributed by Trudy Powers of Sebastopol, CA.

115

Cotton Candy
Country Bumpkin
Cozy Flannels
Cracker Jack
Cream Puff
Crocodile Tears
Cry Baby
Cuddlebug
Cupid's Bow
Curly Top
Cutie Pie
Cygnet
Daddy's Money
Dancing Bear
Dear Diary
Demi-Tasse
Dibbs
Dilly Dally
Dino Soars
Dippity-Do
Ditto
Down Sizing
Dudley Do-Right
Dustbuster

English Muffin
Escargot
Fairchild
Fair-Weather Friend
Fairy Dust
Fairy Godmother
Fairy Tale
Fiddle Dee-Dee
Fiddle Sticks
Fine Print
Flannel P.J.s
Flying Trapeze
Forever Young
Forever Yours
Fortune Cookie
Fox In Sox
Friends Forever
Fuzzy Logic
Fuzzy Wuzzy
Generation Gap
Get Shorty
Giggles
Gimme S'Morze
Gingerale
Gizmo

Goosebumps
Graham Crackers
Grandma's Recipe
Grass Hopper
Gremlin
Grimm's Fairy Tales
Growing Paynes
Guacamole
Gumdrop
Gummie Bear
Half And Half
Half Fare
Half Moon
Half Pence
Half Pint
Half Print
Halftime
Halfway There
Hanky Panky
Happy Talk
Hershey's Kiss
Hidden Treasure
Hip Hop
Hippy Chick
Hobgoblin

Hob Nob
Hobo
Hodge Podge
Hokey Pokey
Holy Moly
Honey Child
Hooligan
Hope Chest
Howdy Doody
Hum Bug
Humdinger
Imaginary Playmate
In Bed By Ten
In Small Print
In Your Dreams
Itsy Bitsy
Itty Bitty
I've Been Grounded
Jellies
Jelly Bean
Jelly Roll
Jiggers
Jingles
Jolly Rancher
Jolly Roger

Joy Rider
Jujubes
Jumping Beans
Just A Little Obvious
Just My Size
Kaleidoscope
Kawabunga
Keepsake
Kibblings
Kidbits
Kid Gloves
Kid's Korner
Kid Napper
Kinder Flinder
King Arthur
King Tut
Kiwi
Knapsack
Knick Knack
Kris Kringle
Lady Bug
Leap Frog
Lickety Split
Lightening Bug
Lil' Abner

Little Annie
Little Audrey
Little Bit
Little Bo Peep
Little Boy Blue
Little Boy Wonder
Little Bugger
Little By Little
Little Chit Chat
Little Critter
Little Debonaire
Little Deuce Coupe
Little Dickens
Little Dipper
Little Dough Boy
Little Drummer Boy
Little Dude
Little Flirt
Little Gem
Little Giant
Little Glow Worm
Little G.T.O
Little Huckster
Little Jack Horner
Little Leaguer

Little Lulu
Little Lord Fauntleroy
Little Man Tate
Little Miss Muffet
Little One
Little Orphan Annie
Little Pittance
Little Preppie
Little Rascal
Little Sheeba
Little Squirt
Little Sultan
Little Thing
Little Trinket
Little Twerp
Little Wise Guy
Lolligagger
Lollipop
Low Profile
Low Rider
Lucky Charm
Macaroon
Make Room For
    Daddy
Malarky

Mama's Favorite
Mere Pittance
Merrylegs
Merry Maker
Micro Chip
Mighty Midget
Mighty Mouse
Mimic Me
Mind Your Manners
Minestrone
Miniscule
Minnow
Minor League
Minuet
Mocha Chip
Mother May I?
Mother's Little
    Helper
Mud Puppy
Muffin Man
Munchkin
Nacho
Nestle's Crunch
Note From Home
Novelty

117

Nursery Rhyme
Nutcracker Sweet
Oh Do Dah Day
Olive Oil
Oompa Loompa
One Hot Puppy
One Small Dime
One Tuff Cookie
Paddington Bear
Party Animal
Patty Cakes
Peanuts
Peek-A-Boo
Persnickety
Pet Peeve
Pickles
Pick Up Sticks
Piglet
Pigpen
Ping Pong
Pinocchio
Pipsqueak
Pistashio
Pitter Patter

Played Hooky
Playmate
Play Station
Pocketsize
Polliwog
Pony Express
Pony Marony
Pony Pepperoni
Pony Tales
Pooh Bear
Popcorn
Pop Tart
Poster Child
Prancer
Precocious
Pringles
Prodigy
Puddle Jumper
Puff
Puff The Magic
    Dragon
Pumpernickel
Puppy Love
Quiz Kid
Rag Doll

Ragga Muffin
Rag Tag
Rata Tat Tat
Report Card
Riddles
Rikki Tikki
Rocky Raccoon
Rootie Tootie
Ruffles
Rug Rat
Rumpelstiltskin
Sassafras
Satin Doll
Scaled Down Version
School Boy
School Daze
School Play
School's Out
School Spirit
Scribbles
Serendipity
Scooby Doo
Scooter
Security Blanket
Sell Short

Sesame Street
Shoe Fly Pie
Shortbread
Short Change
Short Circuit
Shortcut
Short Notice
Short Stop
Short Story
Short Stuff
Short Wave
Simon Says
Silly Putty
Silly Superstition
Skedaddle
Skeeter
Skittles
Slightly Obvious
Small Business
Small Change
Small Fortune
Small Fry
Small Miracle
Small Package
Small Talk

Small Wonder
Small Works
Smarty Pants
Smithereens
Snickers
Snookers
Snookey
Snug As A Bug
Society's Child
Soda Pop
Souvenir
Spinner
Spirit Leader
Spirit Rally
Spoiled Brat
Springer
Sprinkles
Sprout
Sticky Fingers
Stocking Stuffer
Story Time
Story Teller
Sugar Baby
Sugar Foot
Summer Camp

Summer Vacation
Sunday Comics
Sunday's Child
Sweet As Pie
Sweet Dreams
Sweet Pea
Sweet Talk
Sweet Tooth
Taffy
Tattle Tale
Tea Cakes
Teacher's Pet
Teddy Bear
Teeny Bopper
Thanks To Daddy
The Boogie Man
Thingamajig
Three Little Words
Through The Looking
    Glass
Thumbelina
Tickle Me
Tic Tac Toe
Tidbits
Tiddlywinks

Tigger
Tike's Trike
Tinkerbell
Tinker Toy
Tiny Secrets
Tiny Tank
Tiny Tim
Tonka Toy
Toodle-Loo
Toodles
Tooth Fairy
Tootsie Pop
Tootsie Roll
Toy Soldier
Toy Story
Treasure Chest
Trick-Or-Treat
Triggerette
Trinkets
Trisket
Truffles
Trust Account
Tuff Stuff
Twinkle
Twinkle Toes

Twinkle, Twinkle
    Little Star
Velveteen Rabbit
Vignette
Visions Of Sugar
    Plums
Wee-One
Whiz Kid
Wild Child
Wind-Up-Toy
Wish Come True
Yakety Yak
Yoo Hoo
Young
    Whippersnapper
Yum Yum
Zippity Doo Dah

119

Spitfire. Photo contributed by the Belgian Warmblood Breeding Association of Chapin, SC.

BIG & TALL HORSES

A Bit Above
Above All
Above And Beyond
Above Board
Above Suspicion
Above The Law
Above The Rest
Above The Rim
Ace's High
A Cut Above
Aiming High
Airborne Express
Air Raid
Airship
All Time High
Angel In The Skies
Ante Up
Arc De Triumphe
As High As The Sky
A Step Above
Beefcakes
Beluga

Beyond A Doubt
Beyond Belief
Beyond Reach
Beyond Reason
Beyond Suspicion
Beyond The Horizon
Beyond The Pale
Beyond Words
Big Apple
Big Bad John
Big Blue
Big Bopper
Big Business
Big Cheese
Big Deal
Big Dipper
Big Dog
Bigger Than Life
Big Gun
Big Kahuna
Big Leaguer
Big Mac

Big Mama
Big News
Big Secret
Big Shot
Big Sky
Big Spender
Big Surprise
Big Texas Twister
Big Ticket
Big Ticket Item
Big Time
Big Wheel
Big Wig
Bird's Eye View
Burrito Grande
Buffalo Wings
Buns Of Steel
Burrito Grande
Capital Gains
Castle In The Sky
Clipper Ship
Colossal Gains

Corporate Ladder
Defying Gravity
Eight Miles High
Epic
Epic Proportions
Epitome
Everest
Gaining Altitude
Gentle Giant
Giant Peach
Giant Sequoia
Goodyear Blimp
Grand Adventure
Grand Affair
Grand Canyon
Grand Central
Grand Central
  Station
Grand Duet
Grande Dame
Grande Finale
Grand Entrance

Grand Gesture
Grand Illusion
Grandioso
Grand Jury
Grand Larceny
Grand Manier
Grandmaster
Grand Obsession
Grand Opening
Grand Sable
Grand Slam
Grandstand
Grand Teton
Haulin'
Height Of Fashion
Hifalutin
Hi-Fi
Hi Fidelity
High Ambitions
High Anxiety
High As A Kite
High As The Sky
Highbrow
High Class

High Commission
High Country
Higher Ground
Higher Learning
Higher Power
Highest Bidder
High Esteem
Highest Order
High Expectations
High Faluten
High Fashion
High Fidelity
High Five
High Flyer
High Frequency
High Gear
High Gloss
High Horse
High Hopes
High Humidity
High Ideals
High Jack
High Jinx
Highlander
Highland Fling

Highlights
Highly Classified
Highly Motivated
Highly Recommended
Highly Seasoned
High Maintenance
High Noon
High Note
High Octane
High On The Hog
High Pitched
High Places
High Polish
High Praise
High Profile
High Priority
High Regard
High Rise
High Risk
High Roller
High Sierra
High Sign
High Society
High Spirits
High Stakes

High Standards
High Strung
High Tea
High Tech
High Test
High Tide
High Time
High Times
High Tribute
High Voltage
High Yield
High Zone
Hilton
Hot Cross Buns
Industrial Strength
In High Gear
In High Regards
In The Big League
It's High Time
Jolly Green Giant
Jumbo-Sized
Jump Shot
Just Grand
Just My Size
Kingsized

Life At The Top
Lonely At The Top
Long Drink Of Water
Long, Tall One
Lookout Point
Major Scale
Major Shareholder
Market's Rising
Maximum Clearance
Maximum Overdrive
Maximum Speed
Maximum Strength
Mega Bytes
Megahertz
Midnight Snack
Minnesota Fats
Mount Airy
Mount Olympus
Mount Vernon
Mr. Big
Mr. Big Shot
Natural High
No Small Wonder
Over And Above
Overload

Oversize
Pigpen
Pike's Peak
Pillsbury Doughboy
Power Source
Power Surge
Pudgy
Quarter Pounder
Real Big Fish
Really Big Shoot
Really Big Show
Record High
Room At The Top
Room With A View
Search Engine
Seismic Proportions
Simplicity
Skyscraper
Sky's The Limit
Skywalker
Skyward Bound
Slam Dunk
Spandex
Swinging High
Taco Grande

Tall Order
Tall Story
Tall Tale
Tatonka
Thor
Titanic
Titanic Disaster
Top Authority
Top Banana
Top Billing
Top Deck
Top Dog
Top Dollar
Top Drawer
Top Executive
Top Flight
Top Floor
Top Gun
Top Hat
Top Notch
Top Of The Charts
Top Of The Line
Top Of The Morning
Top Of The Wall
Top Of The World

Top Priority
Top Rated
Top Sails
Top Secret
Top Shelf
Tower Of Babel
Tower Of Power
Tunza Talent
Up and Over
Upper Crust
Upper Deck
Upper Echelon
Upscale
Upstaged
Vertical Promotion
View From The Top
Whoppers
Wildebeast
Wilt Chamberlain
World Wide Web
X.L.
X.X.L.
Your Highness
Zenith
Zepplin

Martini and Buddy. Photo contributed by Dawn Lyons of Montgomery, NY.

HORSES WITH ATTITUDE

10,000 Maniacs
Acceleration Clause
Achilles Heel
Adrenaline Rush
Aggravated Assault
Alimony
Andretti
Another Fine Mess
Armed And
    Dangerous
Arrogance
Assailant
Assumed Name
Attila
B-1 Bomber
Bad Influence
Barometric Pressure
Big Bad John
Billy The Kid
Bites The Hand
Blasphemous
Boobie Prize

Born To Be Wild
Born To Fly
Burst Of Energy
Canned Heat
Can't Means Won't
Catch A Flight
Cat On A Hot Tin Roof
Chain Reaction
Chaos
Chemical Reaction
Chili Verde
Cloud Of Dust
Cold Turkey
Combustable
Compulsive Flyer
Conflict Of Interest
Contempt Of Court
Convicted
Cool Your Jets
Cosmic Energy
Countdown
Create A Scene

Criminal
Criminal Mind
Criminal Mischief
Crisis Hotline
Damage Control
D-Day
Deadly
Defying Gravity
Delirious
Delusions Of
    Grandeur
Demented
Dementus
Demons
Dennis The Menace
Departure Time
Destination Unknown
Detention Hall
Detonate
Detour
Devil Dancer
Devil Made Me Do It

Devil May Care
Devil's Advocate
Devil's Deed
Devil's Stardust
Diablo
Diamond In The
    Rough
Different Beat
Different Drummer
Different Perspective
Different Strokes
Double Trouble
Double The Trouble
Driver's Permit
Driving Force
Dynamic
Dynamic Changes
Dynamite
Dynamite Explosion
Dynamo
Edsel
Empty Threat

Energizer
Euphoria
Explosive
Extrovert
Eye Of The Storm
Fairly Hyper
False Identity
Famous Last Words
Farfetched
Far Flung
Fast Forward
Fast Lane
Faust
Faux Pas
Fearless
Fearless Flyer
Fed Up
Feel The Thunder
Fire
Fire Proof
First Offense
Flammable
Flashback
Flighty Flyer

Flying Encounters
Flying Fedora
Flying Font
Flying High
Flying Saucer
Fly Me To Rio
Fly Me To The Moon
Fools Rush In
Forrest "Grump"
For The Heck Of It
Free For All
Free Spirit
Freeway Speed
Frequent Flyer
From Another Planet
From One Extreme
Frostbite
Full Clip
Full Court Press
Full Moon Rising
Full Of Spunk
Full Speed Ahead
Gaining Attitude
Gale Warning
Gallopin' Guru

Gambling Man
Gangster
Geiger Counter
Genghis Khan
Get Outa My Way
Gimme A Break
Ginger Snap
Give The Devil His Due
Goes Ballistic
Gone Fishin'
Gone Postal
Gone With The Wind
Grain Of Salt
Great Balls Of FIre
Gridlock
Guaranteed Fresh
Guided Missile
Guilty As Sin
Hagar The Horrible
Hardball
Hard Copy
Hard Core
Hard Knocks
Hardliner
Hard Rain

Hard Target
Hard Times
Haywire
Heart Stopper
Heat Lightening
Heat Of The Moment
Heat Of The Night
Heat's On
Heat Wave
Heaven Help Us
Hell Bent For Leather
High Anxiety
High Gear
High Jinx
High Maintenance
High Octane
High Powered
High Risk
High Roller
High Spirits
High Stakes
High Strung
High Voltage
Hold Onto Your
    Britches

Holier Than Thou
Holy Cow
Holy Mackerel
Holy Terror
Hooligan
Hot Licks
Hot Potato
Hot Pursuit
Hot Rod
Hot Shot
Hot Tamale
Hotter Than Hades
Hot To Trot
Hot Under The Collar
Hot Wheels
Hot WIred
Hurricane
Identity Crisis
Ill-Gotten Gain
Impending Doom
Impending Storm
Impetuous
Industrial Strength
Indy 500
In Orbit

In Overdrive
Insanity Defense
Insanity Plea
In Sheep's Clothing
Instigator
In The Fast Track
In The Fast Lane
In The Hot Seat
Into Oblivion
Iron Glove
Ivan The Terrible
Jaguar
Jalapeno Salsa
Jalopy
Jeopardy
Jilted
Joy Rider
Jump Start
Justice Due
Just Joking
Killer Instinct
Land Mine
Last Exit To Earth
Lawyer
Lethal Weapon

Listen Mister
Live Wire
Lofty Attitude
Looney Tunes
Loose Around The
    Edges
Loose Cannon
Lost Cause
Lost In Space
Lucifer
Mad Hatter
Mad Scientist
Make My Day
Mars Attacks
Maximum Speed
May Day
Megabuck
Misery
Misery Loves Company
Misguided
Miss Chief
Molotov Cocktail
Mood Swings
Most Wanted
Mount Vesuvius

Moving Violation
My Ex
Nastier
Nasty And Lovin' It!
Naughty By Nature
Nestle's Quick
Next Flight
News Travels Fast
Nine One One
Nitro
No Angel
No Pushover
Nothing To Lose
Notorious
Off The Wall
One Way Ticket
On Fire
On The Fritz
Outer Limits
Out Of This World
Outrageous
Overdrive
Ozone Layer
Pandora's Box
Par Avion

Party Animal
Party Crasher
Pedal To The Metal
Perpetual Motion
Played Hooky
Plenty Of Hype
Poison Arrow
Pompeii

Possessed
Power Bar
Powerhouse
Predicting Storms
Problem Child
Psychedelic
Public Enemy
    Number One

Punchline
Push My Buttons
Radical Dude
Raisin' Cane
Rambunctious
Rampage
Rapid Transit

Rare Form
Raving Maniac
Raw Deal
Red Hot
Red Hot Chili
    Peppers
Retaliation

Johnathon Lobell. Photo contributed by Dawn Lyons of Montgomery, NY.

Revenge Is Sweet
Riff Raff
Ritalin
Roller Coaster Ride
Roman Candle
Rude And Crude
Rude Awakening
Rumpelstiltskin
Rusty Manners
Rush Hour
Satan
Satanic
Satan Spirit
Say My Prayers
Say Your Prayers
Scheduled For
   Take-Off
Schoolyard Bully
Screaming Mimi
Scrooge
Seducer
Semi-Tough
She-Devil
Shenanigans
Shockwave

Short Fuse
Shyster
Sir Dance Alot
Skyward Bound
Smart Remark
S.N.A.F.U.
So Jaded
S.O.S.
Speak Of The Devil
Speed Demon
Speed Freak
Speeding Ticket
Speed Limit
Speed Of Light
Speed Racer
Speedster
Spontaneous
   Combustion
Stage Fright
Street Fighter
Strike Force
Stubborn Streak
Tail Gaiter
Taken For A Ride
Tasmanian Devil

Terminator
The Devil Made Me
   Do It
Thin Ice
Thrill
Thrill Seeker
Thunderbird
Thunder Bolt
Thunder Cloud
Thunderhead
Thunder's Echo
Tidal Wave
Titanic Disaster
T.N.T.
Too Hot To Handle
Total Chaos
To The Limit
Tough As Nails
Tough Company
Tough Cookie
Trouble Brewing
Tuesday's Trouble
Tuff Stuff
Turbo Charged
Turbo Charger

U.F.O.
U.F.O. Citing
Uncertain Times
Under The Influence
Unpredictable
Up In The Air
Volatile
Voltage Regulator
Vroom Vroom
Warlock
Wildebeast
Wild Oats
Wild Party
Wild Spirit
Wiseacre
Wisecracker
Wisenheimer
Wit's End
Worthy Opponent
Zany

EASY-RIDIN' HORSES

Absence Of Malice
Added Comfort
Ain't Misbehavin'
Along For The Ride
Angel In The Skies
An Innocent Man
Answered Prayers
A Real Trooper
Armchair Outlook
As You Wish
Automatic Pilot
Auto Pilot
Autoteller
A Walk In The Park
Backpacker
Backseat Driver
Basic Training
Best Seat In
   The House
Blasé
Bomb-Proof
Camp Counselor

Can-Do Attitude
Candidate For
   Cloning
Cavalier Attitude
Chauffeured Around
Chauffeur Driven
   Ride
Cloud Nine
Company Man
Company Policy
Cool As A Cucumber
Cool Beans
Cool Breeze
Cool It
Cool Jerk
Cool Runnings
Coupe DeVille
Cruise Control
Cruiseliner
Cruiser
Cruising High
Custom Caddy

Custom Made
Degree Of Comfort
De Lorean
Directions Included
Disabled Bomb
Disaster Proof
Dreamworks
Durable Goods
Easy Chair
Easy Choice
Easy Does it
Easy Going
Easy Like Sunday
   Morning
Easy Listening
Easy Living
Easy Lovin'
Easy Rider
Easy Street
Easy To Install
Easy To Please
Easy Touch

Enjoy The Ride
Everything To Gain
E.Z. Ryder
Favorite Easy Chair
Fifth Gear
Fireside Chat
Fleetwood
Fly First Class
Gentle Giant
Gentle Persuasion
Gentle Rain
Gentle Reminder
Genuine
Goof Proof
Goody Two Shoes
Guaranteed Angel
Guaranteed Good
   Time
Guaranteed Goof
   Proof
Guardian Angel
Guidance Counselor

Heaven Sent
Hint Of Heaven
Ho Hum
Hokey Pokey
Honest Abe
Hummer
Icing On The Cake
Instant Gratification
Ironsides
Keeper
Lamborghini
Landcruiser
Lap Of Luxury
Levelheaded
Limo
Low Key
Lucky Number
Luxurious
Luxury Of Time
Luxury Tax
Meditation
My Bodyguard
My Mentor
My R.V.
Navigator

No Problem
Old Reliable
Over Easy
Passivity
Personality Plus
Picture Perfect
Pleasant Company
Pleasant Trip
Positive Feedback
Prescription For
   Stress
Push Button
Rambler
Range Rover
Real Steal
Recreational Vehicle
Remote Control
Rock Of Gilbralter
Run Of The Mill
Safe Ground
Safe Harbor
Safe Haven
Safe Passage
Satisfaction
   Guaranteed

Seventh Heaven
Smooth And Easy
Smoothie
Smooth Sailing
So Easy
Soft Spoken
Soft Touch
Speed Bump
Speed Limit
Spiced Just Right
Spiritlifter
Sport
Sweet Appeal
Sweet As Can Be
Sweet As Pie
Sweet Briar
Sweet Bitters
Sweet Burgundy
Sweet Caroline
Sweet Deal
Sweet Dreams
Sweet Event
Sweetheart Deal
Sweet Pea
Sweet Revenge

Sweet Spot
Sweet Success
Sweet Talk
Sweet Temptation
Sweet Thing
Sweet Victory
The Big Easy
Think Postiive
Town Car
To Your Liking
Training Wheels
Tranquillity
Travel In Style
Two Part Harmony
Ultralight
Under Warranty
User Friendly
Valet Parking
Wake Me When
   It's Over
Walk On Water
What A Breeze
Worth Keeping
Your Wish Is My
   Command

Left: Peregrino. Photo contributed by S. Wilson of the International Generic Horse Association of Rancho Palos Verdes, CA
Right: J. B. Sterling. Photo contributed by American Part-Blooded Horse Registry of Portland, OR.

Colors

Bay & Brown
Bay Colony
Bayberry
Bay Rum
Bay Symphony
Baywatch
Bodega Bay
Brown Derby
Brownie Points
Brown Lightly
Brown Sugar
By The Bay
Cadbury Chocolate
Captain Bay
Cappuccino
Caribbean Bay
Chaleur Bay
Charleston Bay
Chesapeake Bay
Chocolate Brownie
Chocolate Chip
Chocolate Eclair

Chocolate Freak
Chocolate Fudge
Chocolate Irish
    Cream
Chocolate Kiss
Chocolate Mousse
Chocolate Parfait
Chocolate Shake
Chocolate Sundae
Chocolate Swirl
City By The Bay
Cleveland Brown
Cocoa
Cocoa Puffs
Coos Bay
Count Baysea
Creme De Cocoa
Dark Chocolate
Death By Chocolate
Deep Dark Secret
Dipped In Chocolate
Dipstick

Double Fudge
Double Mocha
Dutch Chocolate
Emerald Bay
Espresso
Frisco Bay
Fudge Cookie
Galveston Bay
Galway Bay
Gingerbread Man
Godiva Chocolate
Green Bay Packer
Guantanimo Bay
Half Moon Bay
Hampton Bay
Harmony Bay
Hershey
Hershey Bar
Hershey's Chocolate
Hershey's Kiss
Hot Chocolate
Hot Fudge Sundae

How, Now Brown Cow
Hudson Bay
Humboldt Bay
Instant Coffee
Mahogany
Mahogany Bay
Marble Fudge
Mocha
Monaco Bay
Montego Bay
Monterey Bay
Moonlight Bay
Morro Bay
Mystic Bay
Paradise Bay
Plain Brown Wrapper
Pointless
Sacramento Bay
San Francisco Bay
San Pablo Bay
Santa Monica Bay
Sensational Bay

133

Sugar Free
Sweet Burgundy
Sweet Georgia
   Brown
Tamales Bay
Tampa Bay
The Bay Area
Thunder Bay
Tivoli Bay
Uptown Brown

Ensueno de Colombia. Photo contributed by the Paso Fino Association of Plant City, FL.

Black
Ace Of Spades
Afraid Of The Dark
After Hours
After Midnight
All Decked Out
All Spiffed Up
Art Of Darkness
Back In Black
Basic Black
Before Dawn
Black As Night
Black Beam
Blackberry Jammin'
Black Belt
Blackboard
Black Box
Blark Dart
Black Diamond
Black Forest
Black Friday
Black Fury
Black Gold
Black Hawk
Black Hole

Blackhole
Black Ice
Black Is The Color
Blackjack
Black Knight
Black Label
Black Licorice
Blacklight
Black Limosine
Black Madonna
Black Magic
Black Mail
Black Market
Black Mountain
Black Onyx
Black Out
Black Panther
Black Pearl
Black Reign
Black Russian
Black Sabbath
Black Sheep
Black Suede
Black Tie
Black Tie Affair

Black Tie Required
Black Top
Black Tux
Black Velvet
Black Widow
Boston Blackie
Cadillac Black
Carbon Copy
Caviar
Clint Black
Coal Black
Dark Alley
Dark By Design
Dark Cloud
Dark Continent
Dark Crystal
Dark Reflections
Dark Secret
Dark Shadow
Darkside
Dark Side Of The
   Moon
Dark Victory
Darth Vader
Deep, Dark Secret

Ebony
Edge Of Night
Etched In Black
Fade To Black
Fly By Night
Havannah Nights
Indelible Ink
Inkberry
Ink Blot
Ink Spot
In Spades
In The Black
In The Dark
Into The Night
Jet Black
Karate Black Belt
Knight's Honor
Licorice
Little Black Book
Little Black Dress
Midnight At The
    Oasis
Midnight Clear
Midnight Fright
Midnight Hour

Midnight Madness
Midnight Mist
Midnight Moonlight
Midnight Oil
Midnight Orbit
Midnight Rain
Midnight Rover
Midnight Serenade
Midnight Snack
Midnight Special
Midnight Train To
    Georgia
Midnight Wonder
Nick At Night
Night Affair
Night Call
Night Cap
Night Crossing
Night Delivery
Nightfall
Night Flight
Night Flower
Night Gallery
Night In White Satin
Night Laurel

Night Life
Night Line
Nightly News
Night Magic
Nightmares
Night Music
Night Owl
Night Rider
Nightscape
Night's Glory
Night Shade
Night Shift
Night Train
Night Watch
Night Watchman
Night Worker
Noir Nuit
Obsidian
Overnighter
Patent Leather
Past Midnight
Pinot Noir
Raven
Shadow
Shadow Of Tomorrow

Silohuette
Something Ebony
Something Black
Stroke Of Midnight
Trimmed In Black
Touch Of Pepper
Up All Night

**Chestnut,
Buckskin, Palomino
& Strawberry Roan**
Ace of Hearts
All That Glitters
All The Gold
All The King's Gold
Afternoon Sun
Amaretto
Amarillo
Another Sunrise
Apricot Jam
August Moon
Autumn Colors
Autumn Day
Autumn Hope
Autumn Leaves

135

Colors

Autumn Mist
Available In Gold
Aztec Gold
Bacardi
Banana Boat
Banana Fritters
Banana Republic
Banana Split
Barometer Rising
Battle Colors
Big Red
Bit-O-Honey
Blaze
Blaze Of Glory
Blaze The Horizon
Blondes Are More
    Fun
Blondie
Bloodstone
Bloody Bloke
Bloody Sin
Brass Star
Braveheart
Break Of Dawn

Bright Amber
Bristol Cream
Bronze Idol
Bronze Medal
Bronze Star
Butter Cream
Butterfingers
Buttermilk
Butterscotch
By The Fire
Café Au Lait
California Blush
Capri Sun
Cappuccino
Caramel Chew
Cardamon
Carrot Top
Cast In Bronze
Caught Red-Handed
Cayenne Pepper
Champagne
Champagne
    Celebration
Champagne On Ice
Chardonnay

Chariots Of Fire
Cheap Blonde
Cherries Jubilee
Cherry Bomb
Chestnut Blaze
Chestnut Rapture
Chile Relleno
Cincinnati Red
Cinnabar
Cinnamon
Cinnamon Hill
Cinnamon Stick
Clockwork Orange
Cloth Of Gold
Code Red
Cognac
Coming Up Roses
Controlled Fire
Cool Under Fire
Copper Kettle
Copper Tone
Copper Penny
Coral Beauty
Corazon D'Oro
Country Sunshine

Courage Under Fire
Cranberry
Crème Bruleé
Crème Caramel
Cream Of The Crop
Cream Of Tomato
Cream Puff
Crimson Capers
Crimson Morn
Crimson Sky
Crimson Tide
Crushed Pecans
Dandelion
Dandelion Wine
Dash Of Nutmeg
Dash Of Salt
Dazzle Me Pink
Dijon
Distant Fire
Dressed In Gold
Dun Deal
Dusty Rose
English Toffee
Eternal Fire
Eternal Flame

Every Red Cent
Fahrenheit Rising
Feel The Heat
Feverish
Fever Pitch
Fiery Cascade
Fire And Ice
Fire Cracker
Fire Drill
Fire Engine Red
Fire Escape
Firefly
Fireglow
Fire Marshall
Fire On Ice
Fire On The
    Mountain
Fireball
Firecracker
Firelight
Fire Sign
Firestone
Firestorm
Firewater
Fireworks

Flambé
Flamboyant
Flame Dancer
Flame Thrower
Flaming Ambition
Flaming Fiasco
Flaming Red
Flaming Torch
Flying Ember
Fool's Gold
Forest Flame
Forever Amber
Fox Fire
Foxy Lady
Frappuccino
Fuchsia
Gentlemen Prefer
    Blondes
Georgia Peach
Glowing Ember
Go For The Gold
Gold Bits
Gold Card
Gold Chip
Gold Coast

Gold Coin
Gold Doubloon
Gold Digger
Gold Dust
Golden Apples
Golden Boy
Golden Charm
Golden Child
Golden Dawn
Golden Eagle
Golden Emperor
Golden Fairy Tales
Golden Fleece
Golden Girl
Golden Gloves
Golden Image
Golden Melody
Golden Nugget
Golden Oldie
Golden Opportunity
Golden Pond
Golden Rain
Golden Raindrops
Golden Reflections
Goldenrod

Golden Rule
Golden Slippers
Golden Sovereign
Golden Story Book
Golden Sunshine
Golden Sword
Golden Victory
Golden Years
Gold Fever
Goldfinger
Goldhammer
Goldie Hawn

Martini. Photo contributed by Dawn Lyons of Montgomery, NY. **137**

Colors

Goldilocks
Gold Is Up
Gold Leaf
Goldmine
Gold Nugget
Gold Piece
Gold Reserve
Gold Ribbon
Gold Rush
Gold Seal
Gold Seeker
Goldsmith
Gold Standard
Gold Star
Gold Strike
Gold Watch
Good As Gold
Grace Under Fire
Harvest Moon
Hazy Sunrise
Heart Of Gold
Hearts On Fire
Hello Sunshine
Henna

Hint Of Lemon
Homefire
Honey Grahams
Honey Child
Hot Button
Hot Commodity
Hot Cross Buns
Hot Days
Hot Licks
Hotline
Hot Off The Press
Hot Pepper
Hot Potato
Hot Property
Hot Pursuit
Hot Rod
Hot Shot
Hot Tamale
Hotter Than Hades
Hot Ticket
Hot Toddy
Hot Topic
Hot To Trot
Hotsy Totsy
Hot Wheels

Hot WIred
Indian Summer
Infra-Red
In The Red
Into The Sunrise
Irish Coffee
Jonquil
Justa Nudder
  Redneck
Khaki
Lady In Red
Lemonade
Lemon Chiffon
Lemon Drop
Lemon Meringue
Lemon Parade
Lemon Sherbert
Lemon Springs
Lemon Zinger
Light My Fire
Lightning Strikes
Like Butter
Line Of Fire
Little Red Caboose
Little Red Hen

Little Red Pony
Little Red Roadster
Little Red Wagon
Love Of Gold
Lucky Penny
Maple Sugar
Maraschino Red
Marigold
Meadowlark Lemon
Mellow Yellow
Mercury Rising
Miss Fire
Moment In The Sun
Morning Sunrise
Moscow Red
Moulin Rouge
Mountain Fire
Mr. Goldstrike
Mr. Sandman
Mustard Seed
Native Nectar
Nectarine
Nugget's Karat
Nutmeg
Old Flame

Old Gold
Olympic Fire
On Fire
On Golden Pond
Orange Crush
Orange Marmalade
Orange Peel
Orange Sherbert
Pacific Sun
Paint The Town Red
Panama Red
Paprika
Paved With Gold
Peanut Brittle
Peanut Butter Cup
Pecan Pie
Penny
Penny Candy
Penny For Your
   Thoughts
Penny Lane
Peppermint Twist
Platinum Blonde
Plenty Of Gold
Plum Pudding

Plum Tuckered
Pocket Full Of Gold
Poppy Fields
Pot Of Gold
Pretty Penny
Pumpkin Patch
Pure Gold
Quick Fire
Radical Red
Rapid Fire
Raspberry
Raspberry Red
Ray Of Sunshine
Rebel Red
Red Alert
Red As A Beet
Red Badge Of
   Courage
Red Balloon
Red Baron
Red Bells
"Red" Butler
Red Carpet
Red Carpet
   Treatment

Red Cloud
Red Coats Are
   Coming
Red Currents
Red Eye Express
Redford
Red Fury
Red Handed
Red Head
Red Herring
Red Hot
Red Justice
Red Letter Day
Red Light
Redliner
Red Neck
Red October
Red Rapture
Red Riding Hood
Red River
Red Roadster
Red Rover
Red Royalty
Red Rum
Red Sails

Red Sunset
Red Velvet
Rheingold
Rhubarb Pie
Ring Around the
   Rosie
Rising Fever
Rising Sun
Riviera Sunshine
Rodeo Rosie
Rosebud
Rose-Colored
   Glasses
Rose Is A Rose
Rose Petal
Roses Are Red
Rosette
Rosie Glow
Royal Flush
Ruby Red
Ruby Red Dress
Rusted Through
Saffron
Sandalwood
Sand Castle

Colors

Sand Dance
Sandpiper
Sands Of Time
Sandstone
Sandstorm
Sangria
Scarlet
Scarlet Feather
Scarlet Letter
Scarlet O'Hara
Screaming Yellow
    Zonker
Second Banana
Second Hand Rose
Seeing Red
Sensational Blonde
Silence Is Golden
Silent Sunrise
Silent Sunset
Smoke Signal
Solid Gold
Spark Fire
Speckled
Spirit Fire

Spitfire
Splash Of Gold
Sprinkled With Salt
Spun Gold
Strawberry
Strawberry Daiquiri
Strawberry Field
Strawberry Jam
Strawberry Parfait
Strawberry
    Preserves
Strawberry
    Shortcake
Strawberry Waffle
Strawberry Wine
Strike The Gold
Sunburnt
Sunburst
Sun Catcher
Sundance
Sundancer
Sun Devil
Sundial
Sundown
Sunflower

Sunflower Power
Sun Glare
Sun Glow
Sunkist
Sunlit Glade
Sunny Boy
Sunnybrook
Sunny Came Home
Sunny Delight
Sunny Side Up
Sunny South
Sunproof
Sunrise
Sunrise, Sunset
Sunset
Sunset Beach
Sunset Boulevard
Sunset Delight
Sunset Glow
Sunset Serenade
Sunset Song
Sun Up
Sun Watch
Surefire
Sweet Irish Rose

Tabasco Sauce
Tarragon
Tawny Port
Tendency To Roan
Tequila Sunrise
Terra Cotta
The Red Baron
The Roan Langer
The Sundance Kid
Thin Red Line
Tickle Me Pink
Top Brass
Topaz
Touch Of Gold
Touch Of Saffron
Tow Head
Trail Blazer
Trial By Fire
Turn To Gold
Twenty-Four Karat
Twist Of Lemon
Under The Sun
VISA Gold
Walk In The Sun
White Gold

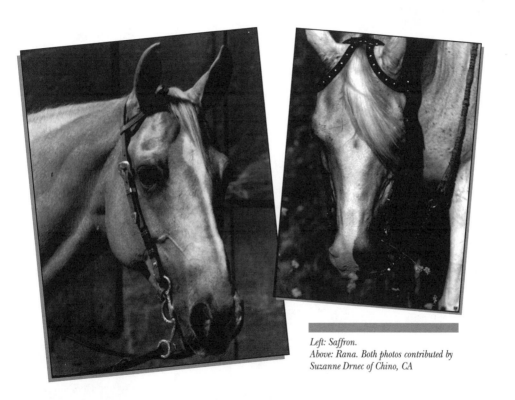

Left: Saffron.
Above: Rana. Both photos contributed by
Suzanne Drnec of Chino, CA

Wild Cherry
Wildfire
Wild Irish Rose
Wild Strawberries
Wings Of Gold
Winter Sun
Yarrow
Yellow Brick Road
Yellow Cab
Yellow Chiffon
Yellow Fever
Yellow Jacket
Yellow Pages
Yellow School Bus
Yellowstone
Yellow Submarine
Young Blood

Grays
& Blue Roans
Aaron Gray
Above The Clouds
Above The Fog
Acoustic Shadow

Alabaster
Alexander The Great
All That Glitters
Another Gray
Antique Ivory
Antique Silver
April Morn
April Shower
April Snow
A Roan At Last
Ashes
Ashes To Ashes
Autumn Mist
Avalanche
Baritone Blues
Battle Smoke
Best Silver
Beyond A Shadow
Beyond The Blue
  Horizon
Blanc De Blanc
Blizzard
Blue Angel
Blue Bayou
Blueberry Hill

Blueberry Muffin
Blueberry Sky
Blue Blazes
Blue Blood
Blue Bonnets
Blue Boy
Blue Chiffon
Blue Chip
Blue Collar Worker
Blue Danube
Blue Denim
Blue Devil
Blue Diamond
Blue Funk
Blue Haze
Blue Horizons
Blue Jay
Blue Jeans
Blue Laws
Blue Light Special
Blue Line
Blue Mist
Blue Moon
Blue Navy
Blue On Blue

Blue Pacific
Blue Plate Special
Blueprint
Blue Sapphire
Blue Shadow
Blue's Harp
Blue Skies
Blue Smoke
Blue Spruce
Blue Stockings
Blue Streak
Blue Suede
Blue Swirl
Blue Velvet
Blue Willow
Blue Yonder
Boogie Woogie Blues
Brilliant Chrome
British Sterling
Burnt Silver
Calm Before The
  Storm
Casper
Chalcedony
Chance Of Showers

Chantilly Lace
Charcoal Sketch
Chase The Blues
Chase The Clouds
Chasing Shadows
Chief White Cloud
China Blue
Chrome Plated
Cinders
City Haze
Clean Slate
Clear Solution
Cloud Burst
Cloud Chamber
Cloud Cover
Cloud Nine
Clouds Above
Cloudy But Clearing
Cloudy Crystal
Cobalt
Code Blue
Confectioner's Sugar
Cool As Ice
Crystal Blue
  Persuasion

Crystal Castle
Crystal Clear
Crystal Delight
Crystal Glow
Crystal Goblet
Crystal Image
Crystal Light
Cultured Pearl
Danielle Steele
Dappled Apple
Days Of Thunder
Dazzled Diamonds
Denim Blues
Denim-N-Diamonds
Dew Drop
Diamond Twist
Dipped In Silver
Done In Charcoal
Dorian Gray
Dress Gray
Driving Snow
Eastern Mist
Earl Grey
Early Winter
Eggplant

Faded Denim
Fairest Of Them All
Falling Snow
First Frost
Five O'Clock Shadow
Fogged In
Fog's Lifting
Forecasting Snow
Forever Blue
Foxfrost
French Vanilla
From Snowy River
Frost Bitten
Frosted
Frosted Mist
Frosted Opal
Frost Fire
Frosting On The
  Cake
Frost Report
Frosty Morning
Frosty Stare
Ghostbuster
Ghostly Presence
Ghost Of A Chance

Ghost Story
Ghost Town
Ghost Writer
Gleaming Glacier
Glitter
Got Da Blues
Gray Ghost
Gray Gleam
Gray Matters
Great White Hope
Grey Flannel Suit
Grey Illusions
Grey Poupon
Grey's Ferry
Greystoke
Grey Streak
Grey Suede
Gunsmoke
Haven't The Foggiest
Head In The Clouds
Hide The Silver
High Steel
Holy Smokes
Home Aroan
Ice Age

143

Iceberg
Icebreaker
Icecap
Ice Capade
Ice Castle
Ice Dancer
Iced Tea
Ice Follies
Ice Storm
Icicle
Icing On The Cake
Igloo
Illuminations
In A Fog
In The Blue
In The Clouds
In The Light
In The Wash Cycle
Invisible Ink
Iron Major
Italian Ice
Ivory
Ivory Coast
Ivory Lace

Ivory Tower
Jack Frost
Knight in White Satin
Lady Jane Gray
Lavender Blue
Leave Me A Roan
Left In The Fog
Left In The Clouds
Light As A Feather
Light Fantastic
Light Stuff
Liquid Silver
Little White Lie
London Calling
London Fog
Long John Silver
Luminescence
Maid Of The Mist
March Frost
Marshmellow
McCloud
Medallic Touches
Medallion
Metallica
Milky Way

Mirage
Misty Magic
Misty Morn
Misty Morning
Moody Blues
Moon Beam
Moondance
Moonglow
Moonlight Shadow
Moonmist
Moonraker
Moon Shadow
Moonshine
Moonstone
Moonstruck
Moonwalker
Morning Cloud
Morning Glory
Mr. White Keys
Mystery
Neon Lights
New Moon Rising
Nickel Silver
Northern Exposure
Northern Haze

Northern Lights
Northern Winds
No Smoking
Not An Appaloosa
Nothin' But Blue
Skies
N.Y.P.D. Blue
Once In A Blue Moon
On Ice
On The Rocks
Opal
Opalescence
Out Of The North
Overcast
Over Ice
Partly Cloudy
Passing Showers
Pearly Gates
Pearly White
Periwinkle
Pewter Power
Phantom Mist
Pinch Of Salt
Pinch Of Sugar
Platinum

Platinum Plus
Polished Silver
Polished Steel
Poltergeist
Porcelain
Powder Puff
Predicting Showers
Predicting Snow
Prism Light
Puff Of Smoke
Pure Cane Sugar
Pure Silver
Purple Haze
Quicksilver
Real Steel
Remington Steel
Rhinestone
Rising Moon
Room To Roan
Royal Blue
Royal Purple
Salt Water Taffy
Sapphire
Satin Lining
Satin Sails

Scattered Showers
Secondhand Smoke
Set In Platinum
Shademaster
Shades Of Gray
Shadow
Shadow Chaser
Shadow Dancer
Shadow Dreams
Shadowfax
Shadow Land
Shadow Of A Doubt
Sheet Music
Shining Armour
Shining Diamond
Silent Storm
Silent Thunder
Silverado
Silver Angel
Silver Armor
Silver Bells
Silver Bullet
Silver By Oneida
Silver Chalice
Silver Charm

Silver Cloud
Silver Coated
Silver Dollar
Silver Edition
Silver Exchange
Silver Fox
Silver Flute
Silver Image
Silver King
Silver Legacy
Silver Lining

Silver Mine
Silver Moon
Silver Palate
Silver Penny
Silver Plated
Silver Runner
Silver Screen
Silver Skates
Silver Slippers
Silver Spoon
Silver Springs
Silver Star

Double Space. Photo contributed by Barbara Mannis of Malvern, PA.

Silver Stone
Silver Streak
Silver Sultan
Silver Sunshine
Silver Tassel
Silver Tears
Silver Threads
Silver Trinket
Silver Tip
Silvery Moon
Singin' The Blues
Slate Sky
Sketched In Charcoal
Sky Light
Smog
Smog Free
Smoggy Day
Smoke Screen
Smoke Signal
Smokey Joe
Smokey Topaz
Smokin'
Smoking Gun
Snowball

Snowball Effect
Snowball's Chance
Snowbird
Snow Bound
Snow Country
Snowed In
Snow Flake
Snow Flurry
Snow Fountain
Snowjob
Snow White
Snowy Day
Snowy River
Solid Silver
Solid Steel
Something Silver
Southern Gray
Sparkling Calistoga
Speck Of Dust
Speeding Bullet
Spilt Milk
Spoonful Of Sugar
Spotless
Spun Glass
Stainless Steel

Stealaway
Steal My Heart
Steal Of The Century
Steal The Silver
Steeler's Wheel
Steel Force
Steel Gray
Steel Guitar
Steel Magnolia
Steel The Silver
Steel Trap
Steel The Limelight
Steely Dan
Steer Clear
Sterling
Sterling Performance
Sterling Reputation
Sterling Silver
Sterling Splendor
Stock Market Blues
Stoneware
Stonewashed
Storm Brewing
Storm Chaser
Storm Clouds

Storm Front
Storm Rising
Storm Warning
Stormy Morn
Stormy Night
Stormy Weather
Sugar Coated
Sugar Daddy
Sugar Mountain
Sugar Ray
Sugartown
Suzi Snowflake
Symphony In Blue
Take It For Granite
Tarnished Silver
Teaspoon Of Vanilla
Tempered Steel
Thunder
Thunder Bolt
Thunder Cloud
Thunder County
Thunderhead
Thunder's Echo
Tiara
Tickle The Ivories

Tip Of The Iceberg
Top Of Ole Smokey
Touch Of Frost
Touch Of Gray
Touch Of The Blues
Touch Of Twilight
True Blue
True Steel
Turquoise
Tweed
Up In Smoke
Vanilla Bean
Vanilla Cream
Vanilla Fudge
Vanilla Shake
Vanilla Wafer
Vanilla Yogurt
Where There's
    Smoke
White Armour
White As A Ghost
White Bread
White Carnation
White Chantilly
White Collar Crime

White Diamond
White Feather
White Fox
White Goblin
White Jade
White Knight
White Men Can Jump
White Out
White Pages
White Sands
Whitespire
White Star
White Wash
White Water
White Water Rapids
White Zinfandel
White Zombie
Wichita Blue
Wild Blue Yonder
Winterberry
Winter Breeze
Wintercrest
Winter Crossing
Winter Fair
Winter Formal

Winter Frost
Winter Games
Winter Gem
Wintermint
Winter Promise
Winter River
Winter Sky
Winter Solstice
Winter Tale
Winter White
Winter Wisdom
Winter Wonderland
Winter Wood
Wintery
Yankee Blues
Zane Grey
Zirconium

**Appaloosa,
Pinto & Paint**

Abstract Design
Abstract Thinker
Abstract Thinking
Achromatix
Acrylics

Adornment
Airbrushed Out
All Decked Out
All Points Bulletin
All Spice
All Spiffed Up
Apache
Arapaho
Argyle
Arpeggio
Art Deco
Art Exhibit
Artful Dodger
Art Gallery
Artistic Impressions
Artistic Interpretation
Artist
Artist's Easel
Artist's Pallet
Art Major
Art Nouveau
Attractive Nuisance
Aurora Borealis
Bar Code
Beauty Mark

147

Beauty Spots
Beyond The Blue
   Horizon
Black & White Print
Blanketed
Blanketed In White
Blind Spot
Blur
Bold Accessories
Bold Design
Bold Destiny

The Sundance Kid owned by Kelly Nelis. Photo contributed by the American Indian Horse Registry of Lockhart, TX.

Bold Impression
Bold Print
Bold Rhythm
Bright Hues
Brightly Colored
Brush Strokes
Burning Bright
Burst Of Color
Calico Prints
Camouflage
Catchy Logo
Cedar Chest
Cherokee
Chicken Pox
Chili Verde
Chips Ahoy
Choclate Chip
Chochtaw
Chipped Paint
Classic Colors
Cloisonné
Cobblestone Street
Collage Of Colors
Color Coded
Color Consultant

Colorfast
Color Guard
Color Me Brave
Color Me Happy
Color Me Purple
Color Of The Wind
Color Prints
Color Sharp
Color Silk
Color Wheel
Complimentary
   Colors
Confectioner's Sugar
Confetti
Connect The Dots
Constellation
Contrasting Colors
Corduroy
Cover Charge
Covered In Spots
Cover My Butt
Crazy Quilt
Dash Of Pepper
Dash Of Salt
Day's Dun

Dear Appy
DeColores
Desert Fox
Desert Storm
Details
Dipped In Chocolate
Dipped In Paint
Domino
Domino Effect
Done In Oil
Dot Com
Dot Matrix
Dotted Line
Dot-To-Dot
Dot Your Eyes
Dress Code
Dressed For Success
Dressed To Kill
Dressed To The Hilt
Dripped Paint
Etch-A-Sketch
Faded Paint
Fancy Duds
Fancy Pants
Fashion Statement

Faux Finish
Few Pointers
Fine Print
Flair For Art
Flamboyant
Flashy Threads
Flying Colors
Forever Plaid
Formal Affair
Formal Attire
Formal Dress
Fresh Paint
Frostbite
Frosted
Frosted Charm
Frosted Flakes
Frost Fire
Frosted Jade
Frosting On
  The Cake
Frost Report
Frosty Stare
Full Color
Gaberdine
Gemstones

Gift Wrapped
Gingham
Goodnight Moon
Go Spot Go
Grafitti
Graham Crackers
Harlequin
Harvest Moon
High Contrast
High Gloss Paint
Hotpoint
Hot Spots
Hot Tip
Icing On The Cake
Illusion
In Black & White
Indian Paintbrush
Indian Summer
Indigo Swing
In Disguise
In Fine Print
In Living Color
In Print
In Small Print
Inspiration Point

In Technicolor
Jackson Pollack
Jigsaw Puzzle
Jambalaya
Keyboard
Kodachrome
Lichtenstein
Living Art
Living Technicolor
Lookout Point
Lots Of Chrome
Lots Of Spots
Masquerade
Matching Colors
Maze Craze
Medicine Man
Metamorphosis
Modern Art
Monogram
Mosaic
Mulligan Stew
Multimedia
Newsprint
New Threads
No Risk Paint

Of A Different Color
Oil-Based Paint
Ol' Blue Eyes
On The Dot
On The Spot
On Your Mark
Optical Illusion
Oreo
Oreo Cookie
Original Art
Ornament
Over Dressed
Overtones
Paint By Numbers
Paint Chips
Paint Drips
Painted Image
Painted Lady
Painted Star
Painted Warrior
Painter's Palette
Painting Spree
Paint Me A Picture
Paint My Wagon
Paint Splash

Paint Splatters
Paisley
Paisley Print
Paper Moon
Pastel Paint
Patches
Patchwork Quilt
Patternmaker
Pebble Beach
Peppermint Twist
Perfect Paint
Perfect Picture
Piecemeal
Piece Of The Puzzle
Pinch Of Cinnamon
Pinch Of Pepper
Pinto
Pinto Beans
Pointillism
Pointless
Point Of No Return
Point To Ponder
Point To Point
Polka Dot

Poker Chips
Portrait Painter
Prairie Colors
Primary Colors
Printed
Puzzled
Puzzle Piece
Reference Point
Rhapsody In Blue
Rorschach Test
Run Spot Run
Rusty In Spots
Security Blanket
See Spot Run
Semi Gloss
Seurat's Dot
Signed Painting
Sketched In Pencil
Speckles
Spectrum Of Colors
Spiced Just Right
Spirit Man
Splash Dancer
Splash Of Color
Splattered Paint

Splotches
Spot Of Tea
Spot Remover
Spots Before
   My Eyes
Spotty Dilemna
Spray Paint
Sprinkles
Sprinkle With Pepper
Still Life Painting
Striking Image
Stroke Of The Brush
Sunday Finery
Sunspot
Take The Rust Out
Tapestry
Tapestry Of Many
   Colors
Tapioca
Tartan Plaid
Technicolor
The Perfect Spot
Three Day Measles
Tie-Dyed
Tonto

Touch Of Spice
Touch Up Paint
True Colors
Tutti Frutti
Tuxedo
Tuxedoed Gentleman
Two Tone
Undercover
Undercover Agent
Under The Covers
Unfinished Painting
War Bonnet
War Paint
War Path
Warrior
Watercolors
Waterproof Paint
Well Decorated
Wet Paint
White Man
White Out
Wing Tips
www dot com
"X" Marks The Spot
Zoot Suit

SPECIAL MARKINGS

Facial Markings

About Face
A Fine Line
A Star Is Born
Among The Stars
Baby Face
Beauty Mark
Belle Starr
Billboard Star
Bio Star
Blaze Of Glory
Blazer
Blazing Bravado
Blazin' Storm
Bless My Stars
Blue Star
Bronze Star
Budding Star
Burst Of Stars
Catch A Falling Star
Catch A Rising Star

Classic Star
Cosmic Star
Co-Star
Delta Star
Devil's Stardust
Easter's Star
Evening Star
Facade
Face 'Em Down
Face In The Crowd
Face Off
Face Paint
Face The Facts
Face The Music
Face The Nation
Face To Face
Face Value
Facing Charges
Facing North
Facing South
Fair Of Face
Fallen Star
Fancy Face

First Star
Flashing Star
Follow The Stars
Freckle Face
Funny Face
Glowing Star
Great American
   Face-Off
Guest Star
Gulf Star
Heading For Stardom
In Your Face
Keeper Of The Stars
Leading Star
Little Star
Lone Star
Marjorie Morningstar
Mask
Masked Fury
Masked Man
Masquerade
Merry Star
Midnight Star

Motion Picture Star
Movie Star
Moving Star
North Star
On Your Mark
Pale Face
Peek-A-Boo
Pokerface
Reach For The Stars
Read The Stars
Right On The Mark
Ringo Starr
Rising Star
Rock Star
Royal Star
Sail With The Stars
Sapphire Star
Save Face
Saving Face
Seeing Stars
Shining Star
Shooting Star
Star Appeal

Star Billing
Star Bright
Starbuck
Star Burst
Star Crossed
Stardust
Starfire
Starfish
Starflight
Stargazer
Star General
Starlet
Starlight Express
Star Light, Star Bright
Starlight Wonder
Star Marine
Star Material
Star Of Bethlehem
Star Of David
Star Of Sapphire
Star Of Stars
Star Pupil
Star Performance

Star Quality
Starry Eyed
Starry Night
Starship Trooper
Star-Spangled Banner
Star Struck
Star Studded
Star Supreme
Star Trek
Star Witness
Summon The Stars
Superstar
That Masked Man
Top Of The Mark
Tristar
Twinkle
Two Faced
Who's That Masked Man?
Wind Star
Wish Upon A Star
Ziggy Stardust

Leg Markings

Argyle Socks
Below The Belt
Bedroom Slippers
Best Dressed
Best Foot Forward
Bobby Socks
Bootie
Bootlegger
Dancing Shoes
Dirty Socks
Fancy Footwork
Fancy Pants
Fox In Socks
Goody Two Shoes
High Heels
Hightop Sneakers
It Takes Two
Knee Deep
Knee High
Knox My Sox Off
Long Johns
Lost My Sock

Mittens
Moccasin
One Shoe On
Pippy Long Stockings
Silk Stockings
Sneakers
Sock It To Me
Stiletto Pumps
To Boot
Two-Inch Spikes
Two Socks
Wearing My Tennies
White Glove
White Sox

HORSES IN PAIRS

Abbot & Costello
Abercrombie & Fitch
Above & Beyond
Aches & Pains
Adam & Eve
Add & Subtract
Advise & Consent
Ajax & Comet
Alfalfa & Buckwheat
Alpha & Omega
Amos & Andy
Anthony & Cleopatra
Anxiety & Phobia
Arsenic & Old Lace
Arts & Letters
Arts & Crafts
Arts & Leisure
Asset & Liability
Astaire & Rogers
Back & Forth
Bacon & Eggs
Bagel & Lox
Bangles & Bobbles

Bar & Grill
Barley & Hopps
Barnum & Bailey
Batman & Robin
Beauty & The Beast
Beavis & Butthead
Beck & Call
Before & After
Bells & Whistles
Ben & Jerry
Betwixt & Between
Bewitched & Bewildered
Bib & Tuck
Biscuits & Gravy
Bits & Pieces
Black & Blue
Black & Tan
Bogie & Bacall
Bonnie & Clyde
Bric & Brac
Bright Lights & City Nights

Buckles & Bows
Bump & Grind
Burgundy & Chablis
Buy One & Get One Free
Cabernet & Chardonnay
Cain & Abel
Calvin & Hobbes
Cash & Carry
Cause & Effect
Cease & Desist
Cha Cha & Rumba
Checks & Balances
Cheech & Chong
Cinnamon & Spice
Clean & Pressed
Clever & Clueless
Cloak & Dagger
Coal & Ashes
Cock & Bull
Coffee & Cream
Coming & Going

Cookies & Cream
Country Bumpkin & City Slicker
Cowboy & Indian
Crime & Punishment
Crimson & Clover
Currier & Ives
Cut & Dried
Cut & Paste
Dagwood & Blondie
David & Goliath
DaVinci & Michelanglo
Daydreams & Nightmares
Debit & Credit
Defense & Prosecution
Democrat & Republican
Denim & Diamonds
Died & Gone To Heaven

Dimples & Freckles
Divide & Conquer
Dollars & Cents
Donner & Blitzen
Doom & Gloom
Dow Jones & Company
Down & Dirty
Dr. Jekyll & Mr. Hyde
Dreams & Wishes
Due & Payable
Dumplings & Gravy
Dungeon & Dragon
Dunn & Bradstreet
Dustbuster & Dirt Devil
Easy Come & Easy Go
Ebony & Ivory
Ego & Super Ego
Error & Omission
Evaluate & Analyze
Even & Odd
Evian & Perrier
Fact & Fiction

Facts & Figures
Fair & Square
Faith & Charity
Fame & Fortune
Fast Start & Strong Finish
Fed-X & Fed-Up
Felix & Oscar
Field & Stream
Fine & Dandy
Fire & Brimestone
Fire & Ice
Fire & Rain
First & Foremost
First & Last
Five & Dime
Flip & Flop
Flirtatious & Bodacious
Flora & Fauna
Foot Loose & Fancy Free
For & Against
Forgive & Forget
Framed & Set Up

Fraud & Faux
Fred & Ethel
Fred & Ginger
Free & Clear
Fun & Frolic
Fun & Games
Fun & Profit
Funk & Wagnel
Genesis & Exodus
George & Gracie
Get Down & Get Funky
Ghouls & Goblins
Gilbert & Sullivan
Gin & Tonic
Give & Take
Glitz & Glitter
Good & Plenty
Greetings & Salutations
Goose & Gander
Goulash & Succotash
Guilty & Innocent
Gumby & Pokey
Gumbo & Jambalaya

Guns & Roses
Guys & Dolls
Hail & Hardy
Ham & Eggs
Hansel & Gretel
Hard & Fast
Hatfields & McCoys
Have & Have-Not
He & She
Heads & Tails
Heart & Soul
Hee & Haw
Hell & Back
Hello & Goodbye
Hemmed & Hawed
Here Today & Gone Tomorrow
Hereto & Therefore
Hide & Seek
High & Mighty
Him & Her
Hit & Run
Hither & Yon
Ho Hum & Diddley Dum

Hokey & Pokey
Hook & Crook
Hope & Glory
Hope & Pray
Hopes & Aspirations
Hopes & Dreams
Huntley & Brinkley
Ice Cream & Pickles
Id & Ego
Iliad & Odyssey
Import & Export
In & Out
Intents & Purposes
Intrigue & Adventure
Intuition & Instinct
Itchy & Scratchy
Itsy Bitsy & Teeny
  Weeny
Jeckyll & Hyde
Judo & Aikido
Jupitier & Mars
Kahlua & Cream
Kibbles & Bits
Kimberly & Clark
Kiss & Tell

Kit & Kaboodle
Lace & Linen
Laurel & Hardy
Law & Order
Lean & Mean
Lea & Perrins
Leaps & Bounds
Left & Right
Levi & Strauss
Lewis & Clark
Lick & A Promise
Little Bit of Rhythm
  & Alot of Soul
Live & Learn
Lo & Behold
Loggins & Messina
Lone Ranger & Tonto
Lord & Taylor
Lost & Found
Loud & Clear
Love & War
Low Key & High Note
Lucky Ducky
  & Lucy Goosey
Macaroni & Cheese

Major & Minor
Mergers &
  Acquisitions
Mondavi & Gallo
Martini & Rossi
Mason & Dixon
Me & My Shadow
Merrymaids &
  Gentlemen
Mesmorized &
  Hypnotized
Milk & Cookies
Milk & Honey
Mix & Match
Mover & Shaker
Muck & Mayhem
Name & Address
Needs & Wants
New & Improved
Nice & Easy
Nickel & Dime
Night & Day
Knick Knack &
  Paddy Wack
Nip & Tuck

Notable & Quotable
Now & Later
Now & Then
Nuts & Bolts
Obsessive &
  Compulsive
Odd & Even
Odds & Ends
Oil & Vinegar
Olive Oil & Popeye
On A Wing & A Prayer
Onward & Upward
Ounce Of Prevention
  & A Pound Of Cure
Partner & Sidekick
Parts & Labor
Peace & Freedom
Peaches & Cream
Peanutbutter & Jelly
Pen & Ink
Pen & Pencil
Pennywise
  & Dollar Foolish
Pick & Choose
Pins & Needles

155

Plus & Minus
Pomp & Circumstance
Porgy & Bess
Porkchops & Spareribs
Pride & Joy
Pride & Prejudice
Prim & Proper
Prince & Pauper
Principle & Interest
Proctor & Gamble
Profit & Loss
Pros & Cons
P's & Q's
Punch & Judy
Push & Pull
Questions & Answers
Quick & Slick
Guilty & Innocent
Raggedy Ann & Andy
Rags & Riches
Rah Rah & Sis Boom Bah
Rank & File

Rant & Rave
Rapids & Currents
Razzle & Dazzle
Ready & Able
Red Hot & Joe Cool
Regal & Royal
Ren & Stimpy
Research & Development
Rhyme & Reason
Rhythm & Blues
Ribbons & Bows
Rich & Famous
Ridicule & Praise
Right & Wrong
Righty Tighty & Lefty Loosey
Rise & Shine
Rising Moon & Setting Sun
Rock & Roll
Rock 'N Roll & Lots Of Soul
Rocket Scientist & Brain Surgeon

Romeo & Juliet
Rosencrantz & Gildenstern
Rough & Ready
Ruffles & Lace
Rum & Coke
Said & Done
Salt & Pepper
Samson & Delilah
Savings & Loan
Saying Grace & Saving Face
Scotch & Soda
Seals & Croft
Search & Rescue
Secrets & Lies
Seek & Find
Seen & Heard
Sense & Sensibility
Short & Sweet
Show & Tell
Shy & Retiring
Silk & Satin
Simon & Garfunkle

Simple Simon & The Pie Man
Siskel & Ebert
Slander & Liable
Slip & Slide
Smith & Barney
Smith & Wesson
Smoke & Fire
Smoke & Mirrors
Smokey & The Bandit
Solomon & Sheba
Song & Dance
Sonny & Cher
Sound & Fury
Soup & Crackers
Sour Grapes & Sweet Pickles
Spanky & Porky
Stable Mable & Black Label
Standard & Poor
Stars & Stripes
Starsky & Hutch
Steals & Deals
Stix & Stones

Stocks & Bonds
Straight & Narrow
Strikes & Spares
Sugar & Spice
Supply & Demand
Sweet & Petite
Sweet & Low
Sweet & Sour
Swing & Sway
Taps & Revelry
Tar & Feathers
Tarzan & Jane
Tea & Crumpets
The Bull & The Bear
The Duke & The Duchess
The Gray & The Blue
The Hare & The Tortoise
Thelma & Louise
The Old Man & The Sea
The Preacher & The Politician
The President & The First Lady

The Prince & The Pauper
The Princess & The Pea
The Young & The Restless
Thick & Thin
This & That
Tigger & Eeyore
Time & Again
TIme & Money
Tinsel & Glitter
Tippecanoe & Tyler Too
To & Fro
Toast & Jam
Toil & Trouble
Tom & Jerry
Toss & Turn
Touch & Go
Town & Country
Trendy & Stylish
Trial & Error
Trials & Tribulations
Tried & True
True & False
Tuck & Roll

Turner & Hooch
Twist & Shout
Two Hoots & A Holler
Two Steps Forward & One Step Back
Up & About
Up & Coming
Up & Over
Uptown & Downtown
Up, Up & Away
Us & Them
Vichyssoise & Bouillaisse
Victory & Fame
Villain & Hero
Vim & Vigor
Vodka & O.J.
Wait & See
Walk The Walk & Talk The Talk
War & Peace
Wash & Wear
Ways & Means
Weights & Measures
Well & Good

What's Hot & What's Not
What's What & Who's Who
Wheeler & Dealer
Wheezie & Sneezzie
Wild & Crazy
Wild & Wonderful
Wild & Wooly
Win & Lose
Windy & Stormy
Wine & Dine
WIne & Roses
Wing & A Prayer
Winnie The Pooh & Tigger too
X-Rated & Parental Guidance
Yankee & The Confederate
Yin & Yang
Yours & Mine

157

MY ALL-TIME FAVORITE NAMES

Write down the most incredible names from this book. Keep them handy for your next horse!

1._____

2._____

3._____

4._____

5._____

6._____

7._____

8._____

9._____

10._____

11._____

12._____

13._____

14._____

15._____

16._____

17._____

18._____

19._____

20._____

21._____

22._____

23._____

24._____

25._____

26._____

27._____

28._____

29._____

30._____

31._____

32._____

33._____

34._____

35._____

36._____

37._____

38._____

39._____

40._____

41._____

42._____

43._____

44._____

45._____

46._____

47._____

48._____

49._____

50._____

51._____

52._____

53._____

54._____

55._____

56._____

57._____

58._____

59._____

Write Us!

💜 **Do you have any funny breed-specific names?** We are working on a second edition of names that will be geared towards specific breeds. Send us your suggestions, names of horses you've know and, of course, your own horse's name! We'd love to hear it!

💜 **Be included in our other books:** Do you have any recipes, grooming tips or handy hints, home remedies, or just comments you'd like to share? Drop us a note, we might use it in an upcoming book!

💜 **Send along funny pictures** of your horse that we can use in upcoming books and newsletters.

💜 **Want to drop a note to the authors?** Send it to Barbara Mannis & Catherine Lewis at the address below.

💜 **Look for Horse Hollow Press books** at your local tack store: *The Original Book of Horse Treats* and *The Ultimate Guide to Pampering Your Horse.*

💜 **Write for our free catalog** of products and books for horse lovers.

HORSE HOLLOW PRESS
P.O. Box 456, Goshen, NY 10924-0456

To order more copies, photocopy this page and mail to the address below. Or, visit your favorite tack & feed, or bookstore!

Yes! Please send me [qty.] _____ copy(ies) of **THE INCREDIBLE LITTLE BOOK OF 10,001 NAMES FOR HORSES** at $8.95 each.

And, I want your other books as well! Please send me [qty.] _____ copy(ies) of **THE ULTIMATE GUIDE TO PAMPERING YOUR HORSE**, a guide to hundreds of handy hints and pampering tips, at $24.95 each. And, I would like [qty.] _____ copy(ies) of **THE ORIGINAL BOOK OF HORSE TREATS**, a cook book of recipes for treats and things I can make at home for my horse, at $19.95 each!

I have included $4.50 for shipping & packing for the first book, $1.50 per additional book. **Total enclosed: $_____** (Check, money order, or credit cards accepted.)

Mail to: HORSE HOLLOW PRESS
               P.O. Box 456
               Goshen, NY 10924-0456

OR CALL TOLL-FREE: 1-800-4-1-HORSE to order!

Name: _____

Address: _____

City/State/Zip: _____

Phone: _____

Visa/MC/AMEX: _____ Exp. Date: _____

Signature: _____